SPRICH DEUTSCH!

A Conversation Manual

Philip Grundlehner
The Johns Hopkins University

HOLT, RINEHART and WINSTON

New York · San Francisco · Toronto · London

Permissions

We wish to thank the following publishers, photographers and companies for permission to reprint material.

German Information Center: 2; Café Glockenspiel: 2 and cover; Hammond Inc., Maplewood N.J.: 6; The University of Munich: 15,16,24; Diener Steinhaus: 31,32; Hotel Haberstock: 56,58; Hotel Vier Jahreszeiten: 56; Stern TV: 64; Thai Tourist Office: 64; HRW: 64; *Praktischen Kochbuch* (Wiener Kirschtorte), Bund Und Zeit: 68; Städitsches Willi-Graf-Gymnasium: 76; Zentrale Transportleitung: 82,89; McDonald's: 112; Volkswagen: 115, 124; Miles Laboratories (Alka Selzer): 116; Josef Guggenmos, *Aus Glas*: 121; Hans Baumann, *Kinderhände*: 122; Mercedes Benz: 123; Porsche: 125; Altmann (Partner Test): 156–157; Monkmeyer: 157; Swiss National Tourist Office: 174; Salzburg Tourist Office: 174

All other photographs were taken by the author, Philip Grundlehner.

Library of Congress Cataloging in Publication Data
Grundlehner, Philip, 1945–
 Sprich Deutsch!

 1. German language—Readers. 2. German language—Conversation and phrase books.
I. Title.
PF3117.G777   438'.6'421   78-23497

ISBN 0-03-022981-2

Table of Contents

Preface

Intended for students with a basic knowledge of German grammar, *Sprich Deutsch!* is designed to encourage oral expression through use of visual cultural material and stimulating conversational topics. Recent and authentic photographs and realia—advertisements, signs, posters, catalog excerpts, menus, recipes and the like—aim to instill in the students an appreciation of contemporary German culture. The carefully chosen topics and questions are intended to help the development of speaking skills with an emphasis on everyday, conversational German.

Uncomplicated dialogues or texts are provided in several chapters to introduce cultural information and present models for vocabulary usage. In addition to content questions (*Zum Besprechen*), more personalized general questions (*Zur ausführlichen Diskussion*) encourage the students to speak about their individual experiences and ideas in relation to the topics presented. Through a wide variety of topics, *Sprich Deutsch!* also prepares the student for either a visit to or an extended stay in Germany.

The text is highly flexible. Units or sub-units can be covered according to individual class interests and time available. There is no progressive degree of difficulty from the beginning to the end of the book, so that topics can be selected at random by the instructors.

A vocabulary list is provided for each photograph or pictorial display to aid the student in answering the questions. Words are listed alphabetically in groups of nouns, verbs, adjectives and adverbs, as well as idiomatic expressions. Principal parts are provided for all irregular verbs. Responses may be simple and straightforward or more lengthy and involved, depending on the imagination and linguistic sophistication of each student or class. Frequently, there is no right or wrong answer. Indeed, the intention of many questions is to elicit as wide a range of responses as possible. Since topics can be selected at random, some high-frequency words are listed more than once. Appendices include an end vocabulary designed to give students the opportunity to refresh their memory on the items learned, lists of irregular verbs, verbs requiring the dative, verbs with prepositions and a table of weight and measurement equivalents.

SPRICH DEUTSCH!

A Conversation Manual

IM CAFÉ

1

Café „Alt-Berliner" —Berlin

Café „Glockenspiel"—Innsbruck

Café „Peterhof" —München

WORTSCHATZ

das Bier, -e   *beer*
der Bürgersteig, -e   *sidewalk*
das Café, -s   *café*
das Eis   *ice cream*
die Erfrischung, -en   *refreshment*
das Filmtheater, -; das Kino, -s   *movie theater*
der Frühling, -e   *spring*
der Gast, ̈e   *customer (in restaurants) guest*
das Gebäude, -   *building*
das Glas, ̈er   *glass*
der Häuserblock, ̈e   *block of houses*
das Hemd, -en   *shirt*
der Herbst, -e   *fall, autumn*
die Jacke, -n   *jacket*
die Jahreszeit, -en   *season*
der Junge, -n, -n   *boy*
der Kellner, -   *waiter*
die Kellnerin, -nen   *waitress*
das Kleid, -er   *dress*
der Kuchen, -   *cake*
die Leute (pl.)   *people*
das Mädchen, -   *girl*
die Person, -en   *person*
die Pflicht, -en   *duty*
der Preis, -e   *price*
der Pulli, -s   *sweater*
die Sahne   *cream*
die Schokolade   *hot chocolate; chocolate*
der Sommer, -   *summer*
die Speisekarte, -n   *menu*
die Steuer, -n   *tax*
die Tageszeit, -en   *time of day*
der Tisch, -e   *table*
die Tischdecke, -n   *table cloth*
das Trinkgeld, -er   *tip*
der Winter, -   *winter*

sich befinden, befand sich, sich befunden   *to be located*
besprechen (bespricht), besprach, besprochen   *to discuss*
bestellen   *to order*
ein·kaufen   *to shop*
essen (ißt), aß, gegessen   *to eat*
fahren (fährt), fuhr, ist gefahren   *to drive, ride, travel (by vehicle)*
gehen (geht), ging, ist gegangen   *to go, walk*
geschehen (geschieht), geschah, ist geschehen   *to happen*
lächeln   *to smile*
lachen   *to laugh*
regnen   *to rain*
schmecken   *to taste*
sitzen, saß, gesessen   *to sit*
sprechen (spricht), sprach, gesprochen   *to speak*
stehen, stand, gestanden   *to stand*
trinken, trank, getrunken   *to drink*
sich unterhalten (unterhält sich), unterhielt sich, sich unterhalten   *to entertain oneself; to converse*

außen   *outside*
gekleidet   *dressed*
inklusive   *inclusive*
innen   *inside*
preiswert   *reasonable*
teuer   *expensive*
wohin   *where to*

sich etwas an·sehen   *to look at something (pictures, menus, maps, studies, etc.)*

1. Wo befinden sich die Leute?
2. Worauf sitzen sie?
3. Sitzen alle Leute?
4. Was steht auf jedem Tisch?
5. Welche Jahreszeit ist es auf den drei Fotos? Begründen Sie Ihre Antwort!
6. Welche Tageszeit ist es? Woher wissen Sie das?
7. Was trinken oder essen die Leute?
8. Wie sind sie gekleidet?
9. Was machen die Leute, die an den Tischen sitzen?
10. Was für Gebäude sehen Sie auf den Bildern von Berlin und München?
11. Wohin gehen die Leute, die nicht im Café sitzen?
12. Sehen Sie sich das Bild vom Café „Peterhof" in München an. Was macht der Kellner? Beschreiben Sie die Pflichten eines Kellners.
13. Was besprechen die drei jungen Mädchen und der junge Mann im Café „Glocken-spiel"? Benutzen Sie Ihre Phantasie!
14. Was würde in diesen Szenen geschehen, wenn es plötzlich regnete?

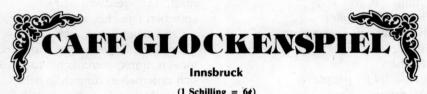

CAFE GLOCKENSPIEL

Innsbruck

(1 Schilling = 6¢)

KAFFEE, TEE		WEIN	
Kaffee mit Sahne	20.—	Offener Wein, weiß 1/4 l	22.—
Espresso mit Sahne	20.—	Offener Wein, rot, 1/4 l	22.—
Tee mit Zitrone oder Sahne	14.50		
Schokolade mit Schlag	18.—		

KUCHEN

aus eigener Konditorei:

HEISSE GETRÄNKE			
Glühwein	24.—	Torten	16.—
Heiße Limonade	15.—	Sachertorte, Käsesahnetorte, Schwarzwälderkirschtorte, Obsttorte, Nußtorte	

KALTE GETRÄNKE			
		Apfelstrudel	16.—
Coca Cola	15.—	Marmorkuchen	12.—
Orangeade	15.—	Pflaumenkuchen	12.—
Limonade	15.—		
Apfelsaft	15.—	**EIS**	
Orangen-Juice	17.—		
Mineralwasser	14.—	Eistorte	15.—
Milch	10.—	Vanilleeis mit	
		heißen Himbeeren	25.—
		Vannilleeis mit	
		Sahne und Waffeln	23.—

BIER

Export hell vom Faß	17.—
1 Flasche Hofbräu-Pils	22.—
1 Flasche HB-Diätpils	22.—

Preise inklusive Bedienung und Steuer

4

ZUR AUSFÜHRLICHEN DISKUSSION

1. Was machen Sie gewöhnlich, nachdem Sie etwas in einem Café gegessen oder getrunken haben?
2. Erzählen Sie, mit wem Sie am liebsten in ein Café oder ein Restaurant gehen.
3. Wohin gehen Sie besonders gern in Ihrer Stadt, wenn Sie etwas essen oder trinken wollen? Findet man auch in Ihrer Stadt Cafés?

ZUM BESPRECHEN

1. Was würden *Sie* bestellen, wenn Sie im Café „Glockenspiel" wären?
2. Kann man im „Café Glockenspiel" preiswert essen? Erklären Sie Ihre Antwort! (1 Schilling = ungefähr 6¢)
3. Muß man im Café „Glockenspiel" Steuern und Trinkgeld (Bedienung) bezahlen? Woher wissen Sie das?
4. Spielen Sie die Rollen von Kellner/Kellnerin und Gast. Bestellen Sie etwas im Café „Glockenspiel".

GEOGRAPHIE

2

Europa

WORTSCHATZ

die Demokratie, -n *democracy*
der Diktator, -en *dictator*
die Diktatur, -en *dictatorship*
der Europäer, - *European*
der Fluß, ⸚sse *river*
die Geographie *geography*
das Gesetz, -e *law*
die Hauptstadt, ⸚e *capital*
die Insel, -n *island*
der Kanal, ⸚e *channel*
der Kanzler, - *chancellor*
der Kilometer, - *kilometer*
der König, -e *king*
die Königin, -nen *queen*
die Lage, -n *situation*
das Land, ⸚er *country*
die Landkarte, -n *map*
das Meer, -e *sea*
die Meile, -n *mile*
der Mensch, -en, -en *person, human being*
die Monarchie, -n *monarchy*
das Nachbarland, ⸚er *bordering country*
der Norden *north*
der Osten *east*
der Ozean, -e *ocean*
das Recht, -e *power, right*
die Regierung, -en *government*
die Regierungsform, -en *form of government*

der Reiseführer, - *travel guide*
der See, -n *lake*
die See *sea, ocean*
der Staat, -en *state, nation*
die Strecke, -n *distance*
der Süden *south*
der Tourist, -en, -en *tourist*
der Unterschied, -e *difference*
der Westen *west*

betragen (beträgt), betrug, betragen *to amount to*
fließen, floß, ist geflossen *to flow*
grenzen an (+ acc.) *to border on*
liegen, lag, gelegen *to lie*
liegen an (+ dat.) *to be situated at*
sich unterscheiden, unterschied sich, sich unterschieden *to differ*
sich vor·stellen *to imagine, to introduce*

nördlich *north, northern, northerly*
östlich *east, eastern, easterly*
südlich *south, southern, southerly*
westlich *west, western, westerly*

eine Reise machen *to take a trip*
miteinander gemeinsam haben *to have in common*

Länder und Sprachen

LAND	SPRACHE	MANN	FRAU
Deutschland	deutsch	Deutscher*	Deutsche
die Schweiz	deutsch (66%)	Schweizer	Schweizerin
	französisch (20%)		
	italienisch (13%)		
	rätoromanisch (1%)		
Österreich	deutsch	Österreicher	Österreicherin
die U.S.A.	englisch	Amerikaner	Amerikanerin
Frankreich	französisch	Franzose	Französin
Spanien	spanisch	Spanier	Spanierin

* **-er** is an adjective ending, i.e., **ein Deutscher** but **der Deutsche**

7

LAND	SPRACHE	MANN	FRAU
Italien	italienisch	Italiener	Italienerin
Jugoslawien	serbo-kroatisch	Jugoslawe	Jugoslawin
Griechenland	griechisch	Grieche	Griechin
England	englisch	Engländer	Engländerin
Irland	irisch	Ire	Irin
Portugal	portugiesisch	Portugiese	Portugiesin
Belgien	flämisch (59%)	Belgier	Belgierin
	französisch (41%)		
die Niederlande	holländisch	Holländer	Holländerin
Dänemark	dänisch	Däne	Dänin
Norwegen	norwegisch	Norweger	Norwegerin
Schweden	schwedisch	Schwede	Schwedin
Finnland	finnisch	Finne	Finnin
Rußland	russisch	Russe	Russin
die Tschechoslowakei	deutsch (4%)	Tscheche	Tschechin
	tschechisch (67%)		
	slowakisch (25%)		
Polen	polnisch	Pole	Polin
Rumänien	rumänisch	Rumäne	Rumänin
Bulgarien	bulgarisch	Bulgare	Bulgarin
die Türkei	türkisch	Türke	Türkin
Ungarn	ungarisch	Ungar	Ungarin

ZUM BESPRECHEN

1. Beschreiben Sie die geographische Lage (a) Deutschlands (b) Frankreichs (c) der Schweiz.
2. Wie stellen Sie sich einen ,,typischen" Nordeuropäer und einen ,,typischen" Südeuropäer vor?
3. Wo liegt das Nördliche Eismeer? Das Schwarze Meer? Das Mittelländische Meer (Mittelmeer)?
4. Nennen Sie die Hauptstädte, die Sie auf der Karte sehen.
5. Was haben Sizilien, Irland und Kreta gemeinsam?
6. Welches ist das größte Land Europas? Welche Länder sind die kleinsten?
7. Nennen Sie einige Flüsse in Europa. Durch welche Länder fließen sie?
8. In welchen Ländern spricht man Deutsch? Germanische Sprachen?
9. Was haben Frankreich und Belgien miteinander gemeinsam?
10. Wie weit ist es von London nach Bonn? Kann man die Strecke mit dem Auto fahren?
11. Welche Länder haben die meisten, welche die wenigsten Nachbarländer? Welche grenzen an mehr als ein Meer oder einen Ozean?
12. Wo liegen Algerien und Tunesien?
13. In Deutschland spricht man deutsch. Der deutsche Mann ist ein Deutscher. Die deutsche Frau ist eine Deutsche. In Amerika spricht man ＿＿＿＿ . Der amerikanische Mann ist ein ＿＿＿＿＿＿＿ . Die amerikanische Frau ist eine ＿＿＿＿ . Nennen Sie anhand dieses Beispiels die Sprachen, die Männer, und die Frauen anderer Länder Europas.

ZUR AUSFÜHRLICHEN DISKUSSION

1. Beschreiben Sie eine Europareise, die Sie gemacht haben.
2. Beschreiben Sie eine Amerikareise, die Sie gemacht haben.
3. Welches ist Ihrer Meinung nach das schönste Land Europas? Warum?
4. Welcher Staat ist Ihrer Meinung nach der schönste Amerikas? Warum?
5. Nennen Sie einige Unterschiede zwischen den Ländern Europas und den Vereinigten Staaten.
6. Spielen Sie mit der Klasse die Rolle eines Reiseführers. Durch welche Länder führen Sie Ihre Gruppe? Warum?
7. Beschreiben Sie die Geographie von . . . (ingendeinem Land).
8. Berichten Sie über das Thema: ,,Die Amerikaner als Touristen.''

WORTSCHATZ

der Ankauf, ⏜e *purchase*
die Deutsche Mark (DM), - *German mark (1 DM = ungefähr 50¢)*
der Geldwechsel, - *money exchange*
der Kurs, -e *exchange rate*

der Pfenning, -e *pfennig (100 Pfennige = 1 Mark)*
der Schalter, - *counter, window*
der Verkauf, ⏜e *sale*

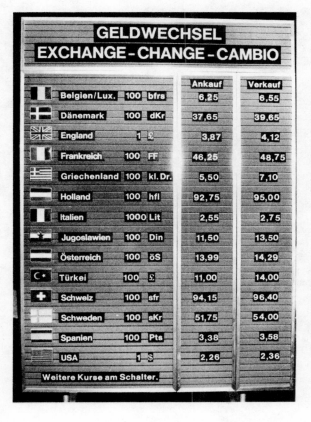

Belgien/Lux.	der belgische Franc, -s (100 Centimes)
Dänemark	die dänische Krone, -n (100 Öre)
England	das Pfund, -e (100 New Pence)
Frankreich	der Franc, -s (100 Centimes)
Griechenland	die Drachme, -n (100 Lepta)
Holland	der Gulden, - (100 Cents)
Italien	die Lira, -re (100 Centesimi)
Jugoslawien	der Dinar, -e (100 Pará)
Österreich	der Schilling, -e (100 Groschen)
Schweiz	der Franken, - (100 Rappen)
Schweden	die schwedische Krone, -n (100 Öre)
Spanien	die Peseta, -ten (100 Céntimos)
Türkei	das türkische Pfund, -e (100 Kurus)
USA	der Dollar, -s (100 Cents)

9

ZUM BESPRECHEN

1. Sie möchten eine Reise von Deutschland nach Rom machen. Wieviele Lire bekommen Sie für DM 2550?
2. Ist es teurer, einen Dollar in Deutschland zu kaufen oder zu verkaufen? Erklären Sie Ihre Antwort!
3. Ist es möglich, japanisches Geld an diesem Schalter zu kaufen? Woher wissen Sie das?
4. Ihre Hotelrechnung für fünf Nächte in Amsterdam beträgt 150 Gulden. Leider haben Sie nur deutsches Geld. Der Gastwirt sagt, daß Sie mit deutschem Geld bezahlen können. Würden Sie das machen? Welches sind die Vor- und Nachteile?

Deutschland

WORTSCHATZ

die Bundesrepublik Deutschland
(BRD) *Federal Republic of
Germany*
die Deutsche Demokratische Republik
(DDR) *German Democratic
Republic*
der Einwohner, - *inhabitant*
die Entfernung, -en *distance*
das Gebiet, -e *area, region*
das Gebirge, - *mountain
range*
die Größe, -n *size*
die Mauer, -n *wall*
der Teil, -e *part*

der Vergleich, -e *comparison*
der Wald, ̈er *forest*

beschreiben, beschrieb,
beschrieben *to describe*
besuchen *to visit*
reisen (ist gereist) *to travel*
verwalten *to supervise*

bevölkert *populated*
dicht *thick (ly)*
geteilt *divided*
wichtig *important*

es gibt *there is, there are*

11

ZUM BESPRECHEN

1. An welche Länder grenzt Deutschland?
2. Nennen Sie die zwei Teile Deutschlands.
3. Wie heißt die Hauptstadt der BRD? Der DDR?
4. Nennen Sie die elf Länder der Bundesrepublik.
5. Beschreiben Sie die Lage von (1) Schleswig-Holstein (2) Bayern (3) Nordrhein-West-falen. Wie heißen die wichtigsten Städte in diesen Ländern?
6. Wie heißen die Gebirge und Wälder Deutschlands? Wo liegen sie?
7. Nennen Sie einige Flüsse und die Länder, durch die sie fließen.
8. Wo liegt Berlin? Wie ist die Stadt geteilt?*
9. Wie groß ist ungefähr die Entfernung zwischen (1) München und Stuttgart (2) Zürich und Frankfurt (3) Freiburg und Hamburg?
10. Wo liegt das größte Industriegebiet Deutschlands?

ZUR AUSFÜHRLICHEN DISKUSSION

1. Sie machen eine Autoreise von Basel nach Hamburg. Sie haben drei Tage Zeit. Durch welche Landschaften und Städte wollen Sie fahren, und in welchen Orten wollen Sie übernachten?
2. Welchen Teil Deutschlands finden Sie am schönsten? Warum?
3. Welche Länder um Deutschland möchten Sie am liebsten besuchen? Warum?

* Berlin wird von den Alliierten des 2. Weltkrieges (England, Frankreich, USA, und UdSSR) verwaltet. Bis 1945 war Berlin die Hauptstadt des Deutschen Reiches. Ost-Berlin ist heute die Hauptstadt der DDR. Seit dem 13. August 1961 sind West-Berlin und Ost-Berlin durch die Mauer geteilt.

Ein Vergleich zwischen Der BRD (62,000,000 Einwohner), der DDR (17,000,000 Einwohner), und dem U.S.A. Staat Illinois (12,000,000 Einwohner)

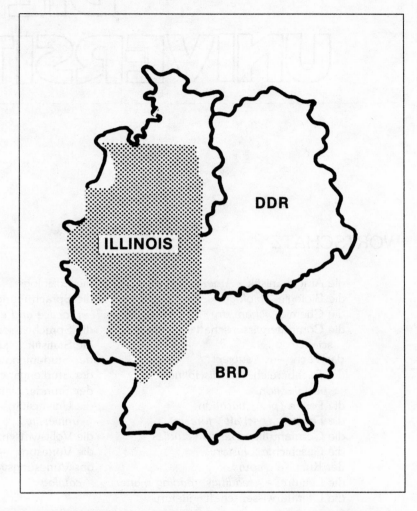

Wie groß sind die BRD und die DDR im Vergleich zum U.S. Staat Illinois. Welcher Staat ist am dichtesten bevölkert?

DIE UNIVERSITÄT

3

WORTSCHATZ

die Amerikanistik *American studies*
die Biologie *biology*
die Chemie *chemistry*
die Computerwissenschaft *computer science*
das Fach, ⁼er *subject*
der Fachbereich, -e *discipline, specialization*
die Ferien *(pl.)* *vacation*
die Forstwissenschaft *forestry*
die Germanistik *German studies*
die Geschichte *history*
der Kurs, -e *course*
die Lektüre, - *readings, reading matter*
die Literaturwissenschaft *literary criticism*
die Mathematik *mathematics*
die Medizin *medicine*
das Pflichtfach, ⁼er *required course*
die Physik *physics*
die politische Wissenschaft *political science*
das Proseminar, -e *proseminar (lecture/discussion usually with paper required)*
die Psychologie *psychology*
der Schriftsteller, - *writer*
das Semester, - *semester*
das Seminar, -e *seminar*
die Sozialwissenschaft, -en *social science*

die Soziologie *sociology*
die Sprachübung, -en *language practice and exercises*
die Sprachwissenschaft *linguistics*
die Statistik *statistics*
der Studentenausweis, -e *student I.D.*
der Studiengang, ⁼e *course of study*
der Stundenplan, ⁼e *course schedule*
die Universität, -en (die Uni, -s) *university*
die Volkswirtschaft *economics*
die Vorlesung, -en *lecture*
das Vorlesungsverzeichnis, -se *course catalog*

auf·stehen, stand auf, ist aufgestanden *to get up*
beginnen, begann, begonnen *to begin*
dauern *to last*
enden *to end*

kurz *short*
lang *long*
leicht *easy*
schwer *difficult*

an der Uni *at the university*
einen Kurs belegen *to take a course*
eine Vorlesung hören *to attend a lecture*

14

Ludwig-Maximilians-Universität
München

Beginn des Sommersemesters	2. Mai
Ende des Sommersemesters	30. Juli
Beginn des Wintersemesters	10. November
Ende des Wintersemesters	20. Februar

FACHBEREICH VOLKSWIRTSCHAFT

VORLESUNGEN:

576.	Ausgewählte Probleme der Volkswirtschaftslehre für Anfänger, 1stündig, Mi.11—12	*Böventer*
588.	Geld, Kredit, Währung, 3stündig, Di.16—17, Fr.13—15	*Gruber*
589.	Budgettheorie, 4stündig, Di.11—13, Do.11—13	*Fecher*
607.	Finanzpolitik, 2stündig, Mi.16—17.30	*Oppenländer*

FACHBEREICH PSYCHOLOGIE UND PÄDAGOGIK

VORLESUNGEN:

1809.	Gedächtnis und Lernen, 3stündig, Mo., Di., Mi.9—10	*Müller*
1812.	Psychologische Aspekte und Probleme der Erziehung, 2stündig, Di.17—19	*Dietrich*
1839.	Sozialpsychologie der Gruppe, 2stündig, Fr.11—13	*Bilden*
1856.	Testtheorie und Testkonstruktion, 2stündig, Fr.9—11	*Franke*

FACHBEREICH MATHEMATIK

VORLESUNGEN:

3047.	Lineare Algebra und analytische Geometrie 4stündig, Di., Fr.11—13	*Prieß*
3061.	Differentialgleichungen 4stündig, Mi., Do.11—13	*Batt*
3084.	Einführung in die Differentialalgebra, 4stündig, Di., Fr.11—13	*Hauger*

FACHBEREICH SOZIALWISSENSCHAFTEN

1. Amerikanistik

VORLESUNGEN:

2863.	Amerika und Revolution, 1776-1979, 2stündig, Mo.11—13	*Wishy*
2865.	Der Tod in Amerika, 2stündig, Di.9—11	*Friedmann*
2867.	Thomas Jefferson: Ideologie und Politik, 2stündig, Di.16—18	*Wishy*
2871.	The Fiction and Non-Fiction of Norman Mailer, 2stündig, Do.18—20	*Ickstadt*

2. Politische Wissenschaft

VORLESUNGEN:

2876.	Marxistische politische Theorie, 2stündig, Mo.9—11	*Adler*
2893.	Sowjetische Außenpolitik 1964 bis heute, 2stündig, Mi.11—13	*Hampe*
2943.	Einführung in die politischen Systeme, 2stündig, Mo.11—13	*F. Schneider*

3. Soziologie

VORLESUNGEN

2961.	Einführung in die Soziologie, 4stündig, Di.9—13	*Recker*
2984.	Zur Soziologie der Frau, 2stündig, Mo.10—12	*Tömmel*

FACHBEREICH BIOLOGIE

1. Botanik

VORLESUNGEN:

3553.	Einführung in die Morphologie, 1stündig, Mo.11—12	*Seibert*

2. Genetik

3593.	Genetik der Mikroorganismen, 2stündig, Do.10—12	*Schweyen*

3. Zoologie

3617.	Einführung in die vergleichende Physiologie, 2stündig, Fr.10—12	*Becker*

4. Mikrobiologie

3689.	Einführung in die Mikrobiologie, Do.11—13	*Fiedler*

FACHBEREICH SPRACH—UND LITERATURWISSENSCHAFT

VORLESUNGEN:

2797.	Goethes "Faust", 2stündig, Mo.10—12	*Motekat*
2812.	Kafkas Erzählungen, 2stündig, Di.13—15	*Nemec*
2833.	Deutsche Lyrik nach 1945 (besonders für ausländische Germanistikstudenten), 2stündig, Fr.9—11	*Henckmann*

LUDWIG-MAXIMILIANS UNIVERSITÄT MÜNCHEN

Studentenausweis (nur zusammen mit amtlichem Lichtbildausweis)

gültig vom 01.04.   bis 30.09

II   Herr/Frau/Fräulein   PK

Tobel Christine

geboren am 11.10.60   in Bremen

ist im **SS**   als ordentliche(r) Studierende(r) an der Universität München immatrikuliert

Fachbereich: Sprach- u. Literaturwissenschaft II

Hochschulsemester: 04   Fachsemester:

Studiengang   DEUTSCH - Hauptfach

ENGLISCH - Nebenfach

Christine Tobel

Eigenhändige Unterschrift des/der Studierenden

ZUM BESPRECHEN

1. Sehen Sie sich den Studentenausweis von Christine Tobel an. Wann und wo ist sie geboren?
2. An welcher Universität ist sie Studentin?
3. In welchem Semester ist sie?
4. Was studiert sie?
5. Sehen Sie sich den Stundenplan von Christine Tobel an (Seite 17). Wieviele Kurse belegt sie? Wer ist Chaucer? Wer ist Brecht?
6. An welchem Tag hat Christine die meisten Vorlesungen? An welchem Tag hat sie die wenigsten?
7. Wann ißt Christine am Donnerstag zu Mittag? Am Freitag?
8. Sehen Sie sich das Vorlesungsverzeichnis der Universität München an (Seite 15). Wann beginnen die Sommer- und Wintersemester? Wann enden die Sommer- und Wintersemester? Wie lange dauert jedes Semester?
9. Wie unterscheidet sich das Semestersystem an einer deutschen Universität von dem an einer amerikanischen Universität?
10. Wann haben die deutschen Studenten Ferien?
11. Was bespricht man in den folgenden Kursen?
    a. Der Tod in Amerika (Amerikanistik)
    b. Zur Soziologie der Frau (Soziologie)
    c. Testtheorie und Testkonstruktion (Pädagogik)

16

CHRISTINE TOBEL · STUNDENPLAN FÜR DAS SOMMERSEMESTER				
MONTAG	**DIENSTAG**	**MITTWOCH**	**DONNERSTAG**	**FREITAG**
8–9 Uhr				
9–10 Uhr			Proseminar: Mittel=hochdeutsche Leküre (*Readings in Middle High German*)	Proseminar: Mittel=hochdeutsche Leküre (*Readings in Middle High German*)	
10–11 Uhr	Chaucer Lektüre (*Readings in Chaucer*)		Vorlesung: Das 15. Jahrhundert in deutscher Literatur (*15th century in German Literature*)	Vorlesung: Das 15. Jahrhundert in deutscher Literatur (*15th century in German Literature*)	Chaucer Lektüre (*Readings in Chaucer*)
11–12 Uhr					
12–13 Uhr		Einführung in das Altenglische (*Intro. to Old English*)	Einführung in das Altenglische (*Intro. to Old English*)		
13–14 Uhr	Vorlesung: Die Werke Brechts (*The Works of Brecht*)		Vorlesung: Die Werke Brechts (*The Works of Brecht*)	Sprachübung English translation	
14–15 Uhr				↓	
15–16 Uhr					
16–17 Uhr					
17–18 Uhr					
18–19 Uhr		Seminar: Gottfried von Straßburg: Tristan und Isolde			
19–20 Uhr					

ZUR AUSFÜHRLICHEN DISKUSSION

1. Wenn Sie einen Studentenausweis haben, zeigen Sie ihn einen Kommilitonen oder einer Kommilitonin. Erklären Sie ihm/ihr die Angaben, die darin stehen.
2. Beschreiben Sie einem Kommilitonen Ihren Stundenplan. Welche Kurse belegen Sie? Wann müssen Sie aufstehen? Wann essen Sie zu Mittag?
3. Welche Kurse aus dem Vorlesungsverzeichnis der Universität München würden Sie belegen? Warum?
4. Welche Kurse möchten Sie nächstes Semester belegen? Gibt es auch Pflichtfächer an Ihrer Uni?

17

Im Hörsaal

WORTSCHATZ

die Bank, ⸗e *bench*
der Hörsaal, -säle *lecture hall*
die Klasse, -n *class*
der Kommilitone, -n, -n *fellow student (male)*
die Kommilitonin, -nen *fellow student (female)*
die Kreide, *chalk*
das Lesepult, -e *lectern*
die Notizen *(pl.)* *notes*
der Professor, -en *professor*
das Schild, -er *sign*
der Student, -en, -en *student (male)*
die Studentin, -nen *student (female)*

die Szene, -n *scene*
die Tafel, -n *blackboard*
die Übung, -en *exercise, class for exercise and discussion*

erwidern *to reply*
halten (hält), hielt, gehalten *to hold*
rauchen *to smoke*
statt·finden, fand statt, stattgefunden *to take place*

eine Vorlesung halten *to give a lecture*
sich Notizen machen (dat.) *to take notes*

ZUM BESPRECHEN

1. Woher wissen Sie, daß diese Übung an einer deutschen Universität stattfindet?
2. Wo sitzen die Studenten?
3. Wo stehen der Professor und die Studentin? Womit schreiben sie an die Tafel?

4. Was hält der Professor in der Hand?
5. Wo steht der Professor gewöhnlich, wenn er eine Vorlesung hält?
6. Was sagt der Professor auf dem Bild? Was erwidert die Studentin?
7. Warum darf man im Hörsaal nicht rauchen?
8. Was machen die Studenten, während der Professor eine Vorlesung hält?

ZUR AUSFÜHRLICHEN DISKUSSION

1. Beschreiben Sie Ihren Deutschlehrer oder Ihre Deutschlehrerin.
2. Beschreiben Sie Ihr Klassenzimmer.
3. Beschreiben Sie die Studenten in Ihrer Vorlesung.

In der Universitätsbibliothek

WORTSCHATZ

die Bibliothek, -en *library*
das Bücherregal, -e *bookshelf, bookstack*
die Kartei, -en *card catalog*
die Leiter, -n *ladder*

lernen *to study (lessons)*
suchen *to look for*

im Hintergrund *in the background*

19

ZUM BESPRECHEN

1. Was machen die Studenten, die an den Tischen sitzen?
2. Wo stehen die beiden Studentinnen im Hintergrund? Was machen sie?
3. Sieht diese Universitätsbibliothek anders aus als die Bibliothek an Ihrer Uni?
4. Was müssen Sie tun, um ein Buch in der Bibliothek zu finden?
5. Können Sie besser in der Bibliothek oder in Ihrem Zimmer lernen? Begründen Sie Ihre Antwort!

Das Studentenleben

Nach der Vorlesung

PAUL: Grüß dich*, Renate. Hast du noch eine Vorlesung heute?

RENATE: Ja. Bis vier Uhr. Dann muß ich büffeln. Ich muß nämlich morgen in meinem Seminar ein Referat halten.

PAUL: Ach, schon wieder. Du bist aber eifrig. Machst du dann im Juli Staatsexamen?

RENATE: Ja, hoffentlich. Ich bin ja schon im zwölften Semester und habe genug Scheine, um mich zum Examen zu melden. Was machst du?

PAUL: Ich bin erst im vierten Semester und mache nächsten Herbst die Zwischenprüfung für Geschichte, mein Hauptfach.

RENATE: Hast du schon zu Mittag gegessen?

PAUL: Nein. Ich gehe gerade in die Mensa. Heute gibt's Bratwurst mit Salzkartoffeln.

RENATE: Und du bleibst trotzdem schlank. Ich muß leider auf so viele Kalorien verzichten, sonst werde ich dick.

PAUL: Ach wo, du bist doch schön schlank, Mädchen. Kommst du mit?

RENATE: Ja, aber ich habe meinen Studentenausweis vergessen und kann deshalb keine Essenmünze kaufen.

PAUL: Ich schenk' dir eine. Sie kostet nur eine Mark achtzig.

RENATE: Das ist sehr nett von dir. Trinkst du morgen ein Bierchen mit mir nach meinem Referat?

PAUL: Ja, gerne. Dann können wir auf mein Zimmer im Verbindungshaus gehen.

RENATE: Zu welcher Verbindung gehörst du denn?

PAUL: Zur Suevia in der Blütenstraße.

RENATE: Ich bringe eine Flasche Wein und mein neues Fleetwood Mac Album mit.

PAUL: Schön, Renate. Gehen wir jetzt essen!

WORTSCHATZ

das Album, -ben (record) album
die Essenmünze, -n (also: Essenmarke)
  coin purchased for meal in the
  "Mensa"
das Hauptfach, ⁼er major
die Kalorie, -n calorie
der Klassenkamerad, -en, -
  en classmate
Lieblings, - favorite
die Mensa, - -sen university cafeteria
das Nebenfach, ⁼er academic minor
das Referat, -e oral and written paper
die Salzkartoffeln (pl.) boiled potatoes
das Semester, - semester
das Seminar, -e seminar
das Staatsexamen, -ina state exam
  (final exam before graduation for
  German univ. students)
das Studienbuch, ⁼er record book of
  courses taken at a German university
das Verbindungshaus, ⁼er fraternity
  house

die Vorlesung, -en lecture, lecture
  course
die Zwischenprüfung, -en mid-
  curriculum exam

büffeln to cram
gehören zu to belong to
grüßen to greet
mit·bringen, brachte mit,
  mitgebracht to bring along
schenken to present, give
schwänzen to cut class
verzichten auf (+ acc.) to forgo
  something

deshalb therefore
dick fat
eifrig ambitious
gerade directly, straight
hoffentlich hopefully
leider unfortunately
nämlich namely
schlank slender

22

ein Examen, eine Prüfung bestehen
bestand, bestanden *to pass an
exam, a test*

ein Examen, eine Prüfung machen *to
take an exam, a test*

ein „Bierchen" trinken gehen *to go
for a beer*

erst nächsten Herbst *not until next fall*

in einem Examen (einer Prüfung)
durch·fallen (fällt durch) fiel durch, ist
durchgefallen *to fail an exam (a
test)*

sich zum Examen melden *to apply to
take an exam*

zu Mittag essen *to eat lunch*

ZUM BESPRECHEN

1. Warum muß Renate büffeln?
2. Warum macht Renate ihr Staatsexamen im Juli?
3. Wie weit ist Paul mit seinem Studium?
4. Warum ißt Renate keine Wurst oder keine Kartoffeln?
5. Wieso kann Renate keine Essenmünze kaufen?
6. Was machen Renate und Paul nach Renates Referat?

ZUR AUSFÜHRLICHEN DISKUSSION

1. Was ist Ihr Hauptfach? Ihr Nebenfach?
2. Wie oft müssen Sie büffeln? Wie oft haben Sie schon Ihre Vorlesungen und Übungen geschwänzt?
3. Geben Sie einige Tips, wie man eine schwere Prüfung besteht.
4. Beschreiben Sie einen Kurs oder eine Prüfung, in der Sie fast durchgefallen sind.
5. Spielen Sie die Rolle eines deutschen Studenten in Amerika. Stellen Sie Ihren amerikanischen Kommilitonen Fragen über das Studium in Amerika.
6. Beschreiben Sie Ihre Lieblingsvorlesung!

23

In der Mensa

STUDENTENWERK MÜNCHEN	MENSA UNIVERSITÄT

TAGESKARTE FÜR MONTAG, DEN 06.06.		
MITTAGESSEN	STAMMESSEN -DM 1,80 (complete meal, table d' hôte)	ANZAHL KALORIEN
	BIERWURST (cold cut)	495
	BRATENSAUCE (gravy)	77
	GRÜNER SALAT (green salad)	75
	SALZKARTOFFELN (boiled potatoes)	213
	APFELKALTSCHALE (cold apple soup)	140
MITTAGESSEN	AUSWAHLESSEN -DM 2,80 (à la carte)	ANZAHL KALORIEN
	NUDELSUPPE	126
	SCHWEINSKOTELETT (pork chops)	609
	HÄHNCHENSCHNITZEL PANIERT (fried chicken)	370
	TIROLER SAUCE (sauce tyrolienne)	229
	GURKENSALAT (cucumber salad)	57
	BOHNENSALAT (bean salad)	87
	GRÜNER SALAT MIT EIERDRESSING (Boston lettuce with egg dressing)	68
	REIS (rice)	290
	KROKETTEN (croquettes)	204
	KARTOFFELBREI (mashed potatoes)	180
	QUARKSPEISE MIT BLAUBEEREN (similar to yogurt with blueberries)	138
	KÜRBISKOMPOTT (pumpkin compote)	102

WORTSCHATZ

die Anzahl *number*

das Auswahlessen, - *meal where student can select from choices available*

das Mittagessen, - *lunch*

der Schein, -e *bill (money note)*

das Studentenwerk, -e *student union*

vor·ziehen, zog vor, vorgezogen *to prefer*

In der Mensa

ZUM BESPRECHEN _____

1. Beschreiben Sie den Unterschied zwischen dem Stammessen und dem Auswahlessen.
2. Sehen Sie sich das Foto an. Was muß der Student tun, bevor er sein Essen bekommen kann?
3. Sie haben einen Zehnmarkschein. Spielen Sie mit einem Kommilitonen die Rollen von Münzenverkäuferin und Studenten (Studentin).
4. Für welches Essen würden Sie Marken kaufen? Warum?

ZUR AUSFÜHRLICHEN DISKUSSION _____

1. Gibt es auch in Ihrer Mensa ein Stammessen und ein Auswahlessen?
2. Beschreiben Sie das Essen in Ihrer Mensa.
3. Essen Sie lieber in der Mensa oder zu Hause? Warum?

25

Beschreiben Sie dieses Bild vor dem Studentenwerk der Universität München.

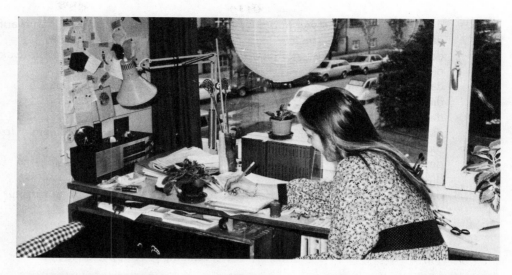

Im Studentenheim

WORTSCHATZ

das Armband, ⁼er   *bracelet*
der Bleistift, -e   *pencil*
das schwarze Brett, -er   *bulletin board*
die Decke, -n   *cover, blanket*
das Fenster, -   *window*
der Gegenstand, ⁼e   *object*
das Glas, ⁼er   *glass*
das Heft, -e   *notebook*
die Hose, -n   *trousers*

der Kugelschreiber, - (der Kuli, -
  s)   *ballpoint pen*
die Lampe, -n   *lamp*
das Licht, -er   *light*
die Pfeife, -n   *pipe*
die Pflanze, -n   *plant*
das Radio, -s   *radio*
der Schachbrett, -er   *chess board*
die Schere, -n   *scissors*

27

das Stockwerk, -e *story, floor*
das Streichholz, ⸚er *match*
das Studentenheim, -e *dormitory*[1]
der Stuhl, ⸚e *chair*
das Tonbandgerät, ⸚e *tape recorder*
die Uhr, -en *clock*
der Vorhang, ⸚e *curtain*
die Wand, ⸚e *wall*
die Wohnung, -en *apartment*
der Zettel, - *note*
die Zigarette, -n *cigarette*
das Zimmer, - *room*
der Zimmerkollege, -n *roommate (male)*[2]
die Zimmerkollegin, -nen *roommate (female)*[2]

an·hören *to listen to*
arbeiten an (+ acc.) *to work on*

auf·nehmen (nimmt auf), nahm auf, aufgenommen *to record*
auf·wachen ist aufgewacht *to wake up*
hängen an (+ acc.) *to attach to*
hören *to hear*
rauchen *to smoke*
schreiben, schrieb, geschrieben *to write*
sitzen, saß, gesessen *to sit*
spielen *to play*
studieren *to study (at a university)*

ordentlich *tidy*
pünktlich *punctual(ly)*
schlampig *sloppy, untidy*

ZUM BESPRECHEN

1. Womit schreibt der Student? Die Studentin?
2. Woran arbeiten sie wahrscheinlich?
3. Beschreiben Sie die Kleidung der zwei Studenten.
4. Warum haben die beiden Studenten Wecker auf ihren Tischen?
5. Sind die Zimmer der Studenten ordentlich oder schlampig?
6. Rauchen die beiden Studenten? Woher wissen Sie das?
7. Woran hat die Studentin die vielen Zettel gehängt? Was könnte auf diesen Zetteln stehen?
8. In welchem Stockwerk wohnt die Studentin? Woher wissen Sie das?
9. Was liegt auf dem Bett des Studenten?
10. Was nimmt der Student mit seinem Tonbandgerät wahrscheinlich auf?

ZUR AUSFÜHRLICHEN DISKUSSION

1. Welche Gegenstände, die Sie auf den Bildern sehen, haben Sie auch in Ihrem Zimmer?
2. Ist Ihr Zimmer schlampig oder ordentlich?
3. Beschreiben Sie Ihren Zimmerkollegen oder Ihre Zimmerkollegin.
4. Beschreiben Sie das Leben in Ihrem Studentenheim.
5. Ziehen Sie es vor, im Studentenheim, im Verbindungshaus, oder in einer Privatwohnung in der Nähe der Universität zu wohnen? Warum?

[1] Dorms in Germany usually are coed and have a kitchen on each floor. There are no parietal hours, alcohol is not prohibited, and there is no resident adviser.

[2] German students usually live in single rooms.

Im Studentenlokal

WORTSCHATZ

der Bierkeller, - *pub*
das Lokal, -e *tavern*
der Krug, ⸚e *mug, pitcher*
die Maß, - *liter of beer*

an·stoßen (stößt an), stieß an,
  angestoßen *to clink glasses (as in a
  toast)*
sich betrinken, betrank sich, sich
  betrunken *to get drunk*
sich freuen *to be happy*

angeheitert *slightly tipsy, "mellow"*
blau *drunk, "plastered"*
nüchtern *sober*

auf deine Gesundheit an·stoßen *to
  drink to your health*
Pros(i)t! *Cheers!*

ZUM BESPRECHEN

1. Wo befinden sich die Studenten?
2. Was machen die Studenten auf dem Bild?
3. Was trinken die Studenten? Was halten sie in den Händen?

29

4. Wieviel Bier ist in jedem Krug?
5. Was sagen sie, wenn sie anstoßen?
6. Worüber reden die Studenten, die am Tisch sitzen?
7. Wie sagt man, *I drink to your health!*?

ZUR AUSFÜHRLICHEN DISKUSSION

1. Was machen Sie normalerweise am Abend, wenn Sie von der Uni kommen?
2. Beschreiben Sie Ihr Lieblingslokal.
3. Gehen Sie lieber mit einer Gruppe Mädchen oder einer Gruppe Jungen aus? Warum?
4. Wie benehmen Sie sich, wenn Sie angeheitert sind?

DAS HAUS

WORTSCHATZ

die Antenne, -n *antenna*
der Balkon, -e *balcony*
das Dach, ̈er *roof*
die Dachrinne, -n *gutter*
der Garten, ̈ *garden, yard (front and back)*

die Lampe, -n *lamp*
der Schornstein, -e *chimney*
die Terrasse, -n *terrace*
der Vorhang, ̈e *curtain*

ZUM BESPRECHEN

1. Vergleichen Sie das deutsche Haus auf Seite 31 mit amerikanischen Häusern.
2. Wozu braucht man eine Antenne auf dem Dach?
3. Warum ist es schön, einen Balkon zu haben?
4. Wozu dient die Lampe an der Terrassenwand?
5. Wieso braucht ein Haus immer einen Schornstein?
6. Beschreiben Sie den Garten Ihres Hauses.

ERDGESCHOSS

OBERGESCHOSS

KELLER

Das Innere des Hauses

WORTSCHATZ

das Arbeitszimmer, - *study*
das Bad, ¨er *bathroom*
der Beistelltisch, -e *side table*
das Bett, -en *bed*
der Couchtisch, -e *coffee table*
der Einbauschrank, ¨e *closet*
die Eltern (*pl.*) *parents*
das Erdgeschoß, -sse *ground floor*
das Eßzimmer, - *dining room*

die Etage, -n *floor*
der Flur, -e *hall*
die Garage, -n *garage*
die Garderobe, -n *hall closet, part of foyer used to hang up coats*
das Gästezimmer, - *guest room*
die Heizung, -en *heater, heating*
das Innere *interior*
der Kamin, -e *fireplace*

der Keller, - *cellar*
der Kleiderschrank, ⸚e *wardrobe*
die Küche, -n *kitchen*
die Möbel (*pl.*) *furniture*
das Möbelstück, ⸚e *piece of furniture*
der Nachttisch, -e *night table*
das Obergeschoß, -sse *second story*
  (**Geschoß** cannot be used for floors
  higher than the second.)
der Sessel, - *armchair*
das Sofa, -s *sofa*
der Stuhl, ⸚e *chair*
der Tank, -s *tank*
die Toilette, -n, das WC, -s *toilet*
die Treppe, -n *stairs*
der Trockner, - *dryer*
die Waschküche, -n *washer-dryer
  area, area to hang up clothes to dry*

die Waschmaschine, -n *washing-
  machine*
die Wohnwand, ⸚e *wall-length set of
  cabinets for living room (see picture)*

erledigen *to take care of, execute*
grillen *to barbecue, grill*
mieten *to rent*
putzen *to clean*
trocknen *to dry*
verbringen, verbrachte, verbracht *to
  spend (time)*
waschen (wäscht), wusch,
  gewaschen *to wash*

zu Hause *at home*

die Wohnwand

ZUM BESPRECHEN

1. Wieviele Stockwerke hat dieses Haus (Seite 32)? Nennen Sie die Zimmer in jedem Stockwerk.
2. Welches ist das größte Zimmer im Haus? Warum?
3. Beschreiben Sie die Familie, die in diesem Haus wohnt.
4. Welche Möbelstücke sind im Wohnzimmer?
5. Welche Möbelstücke sind in den Schlafzimmern? Was stellt man normalerweise auf den Nachttisch? Hat jedes Schlafzimmer einen Einbauschrank wie in einem amerikanischen Haus?
6. Wäre die Garage in diesem Haus groß genug für Ihre Familie?
7. Wo ist die Waschküche? Was steht darin? Was macht man dort?
8. Was kann man aus den Kellerräumen machen?

33

9. Welche Arbeiten erledigt man gewöhnlich im Arbeitszimmer?
10. Wozu braucht man einen Tank im Keller?
11. Wo gibt es Platz zum Grillen?
12. Hat dieses Haus einen Kamin? Wo? Warum ist es schön, einen Kamin zu haben?

ZUR AUSFÜHRLICHEN DISKUSSION

1. Möchten Sie in diesem Haus wohnen? Warum oder warum nicht?
2. Beschreiben Sie der Klasse Ihr Haus und die Zimmer darin.
3. Möchten Sie lieber ein Haus kaufen oder mieten? Warum?
4. Essen Sie zu Hause in der Küche oder im Eßzimmer?
5. Beschreiben Sie Ihr Zimmer zu Hause.
6. In welchem Zimmer Ihres Hauses verbringen Sie die meiste Zeit? Warum?
7. Wer putzt bei Ihnen zu Hause? Wie oft muß man das tun?

Die Küche

WORTSCHATZ

34

der Ausguß ̈-sse *sink*
der Backofen, ̈ *oven*
das Besteck, -e *knives, forks and
    spoons; cutlery, silverware*

die Gabel, -n *fork*
das Geschirr *dishes*
die Geschirrspülmaschine, -n
    dishwasher

das Glas, ⸚er *glass*
das Handrührgerät, -e *mixer*
der Herd, -e *stove*
die Herdplatte, -n *burner*
der Kaffeeautomat, -en *coffeemaker*
die Küche, -n *kitchen*
der Kühlschrank, ⸚e *refrigerator*
der Löffel, - *spoon*
das Messer, - *knife*
die Schublade, -n *drawer*
die Steckdose, -n *electrical outlet*
der Teller, - *plate*
der Toaster, - *toaster*

der Topf, ⸚e *pot*
der Topflappen, - *pot holder*

backen (bäckt), backte, gebacken *to bake*
braten (brät), briet, gebraten *to roast*
ein·stecken *to plug in*
kochen *to cook*
spülen *to wash dishes*
toasten *to toast*

modern *modern*
vollständig *complete(ly)*

ZUM BESPRECHEN

1. Beschreiben Sie das Bild so vollständig wie möglich. Woran sehen Sie, daß diese Küche modern ist?
2. Was legt man in die Küchenschränke und die Schubladen?
3. Benutzt die Frau auf dem Foto den Backofen? Woran sehen Sie das?
4. Wozu braucht man einen Topflappen?
5. Wo sieht man eine Steckdose auf dem Bild? Wozu braucht man Steckdosen in der Küche?
6. Beschreiben Sie den Unterschied zwischen ,,kochen", ,,backen" und ,,braten".

ZUR AUSFÜHRLICHEN DISKUSSION

1. Beschreiben Sie Ihre Küche zu Hause.
2. Sind Sie der Meinung, daß die Hausfrau immer kochen und spülen sollte? Warum oder warum nicht?
3. Vergleichen Sie diese deutsche mit einer amerikanischen Küche.
4. Erklären Sie den Satz ,,Die Arbeit einer Hausfrau ist nie zu Ende".

35

Das Badezimmer

WORTSCHATZ

die Badewanne, -n *bathtub*
die Dusche, -n *shower*
die Handdusche, -n *hand shower*
die Toilette, -n; *toilet*
die Waage, -n *scale*
das Waschbecken, - *sink*

baden *to bathe*
sich duschen *to take a shower*
sich kämmen *to comb one's hair*
vergleichen, verglich, verglichen *to compare*

sich waschen (wäscht sich), wusch sich, sich gewaschen *to wash oneself*
sich wiegen, wog sich, sich gewogen *to weigh oneself*

auf die Toilette gehen *to go to the bathroom*
sich die Zähne putzen *to brush one's teeth*
Toilette machen *to get dressed*

ZUM BESPRECHEN

1. Was tut das Mädchen auf dem Bild?
2. Warum sind in diesem Badezimmer zwei Waschbecken?
3. Was ist der Unterschied zwischen einer Handdusche und einer Dusche? Was für eine Dusche sehen Sie auf dem Foto?
4. Warum steht in dem Badezimmer eine Waage?
5. Wie sagt man auf deutsch *I have to go to the bathroom?*
6. Vergleichen Sie das deutsche und das amerikanische Badezimmer.

36

ZUR AUSFÜHRLICHEN DISKUSSION

1. Beschreiben Sie den Unterschied zwischen einem W.C. (einer Toilette) und einem Badezimmer.
2. Wie oft sollte man sich die Zähne putzen? Warum? Wie oft putzen Sie sich die Zähne?
3. Was tun Sie lieber? Duschen oder baden? Warum?

Das Schlafzimmer

WORTSCHATZ

die Bettwäsche *bed linen*
die Decke, -n *blanket*
das Federbett, -en *feather bed*
das Kissen, - *pillow*
der Spiegel, - *mirror*
der Wecker, - *alarm clock*

auf·stehen, stand auf, ist aufgestanden *to get up*

auf·wachen, ist aufge·wacht *to awaken*
schlafen (schläft), schlief, geschlafen *to sleep*

am Wochenende *on the weekend*
ins Bett gehen *to go to bed*
jeden Tag *every day*
um wieviel Uhr *at what time*

37

ZUM BESPRECHEN

1. Beschreiben Sie das Bild.
2. Wie unterscheidet sich die Bettwäsche in Deutschland von der in Amerika?
3. Wozu braucht man einen Spiegel und einen Wecker im Schlafzimmer?

ZUR AUSFÜHRLICHEN DISKUSSION

1. Um wieviel Uhr gehen Sie abends ins Bett? Bis wann schlafen Sie normalerweise am Morgen? Stehen Sie am Wochenende früh auf? Warum oder warum nicht?
2. Beschreiben Sie Ihr Schlafzimmer zu Hause.
3. Brauchen Sie immer einen Wecker, um aufzuwachen?

IN DER STADT

5

Eine Stadtführung

Hier beginnt die Stadtführung
SIGHT
SEEING
Preis: S 35.- DM 5.-
Programm:

WORTSCHATZ

der Architekt, -en, -en *architect*
der Arzt, ⸚e *physician (male)*
die Ärztin, -nen *physician (female)*
der Bankier, -s *banker*
der Bürgermeister, - *mayor*
der Gastwirt, -e *innkeeper*
die Heimatstadt, ⸚e *native city*
der Ladenbesitzer, - *shop owner*
die Lieblingsstadt, ⸚e *favorite city*

der Polizist, -en, -en *policeman*
der Rechtsanwalt, ⸚e *attorney*
der Schuldirektor, -en *school principal*
die Stadtführung, -en *city tour*

vertreten (vertritt), vertrat, vertreten *to represent*
zeichnen *to draw*

39

ZUM BESPRECHEN

1. Machen Sie mit Ihrem Kommilitonen eine Führung durch Ihre Heimatstadt.
2. Beschreiben Sie Ihre Lieblingsstadt.
3. Planen Sie in Ihrer Klasse eine ideale Stadt. Jeder Student soll einen Beruf vertreten, z.B.
   Bürgermeister, Polizist, verschiedene Ladenbesitzer, Architekt, Schuldirektor, Bankier, Rechtsanwalt, Arzt, Gastwirt usw.
   Benutzen Sie die Tafel, um den Stadtplan zu zeichnen.

40

An der Bushaltestelle

Stadtbahn

 Haltestelle

 Untergrundbahn

 Einfahrt verboten

WORTSCHATZ

der (Auto)bus, -se *bus*
der Bürgersteig, -e *sidewalk*
die Ecke, -n *corner*
die Einbahnstraße, -n *one-way street*
der Fußgänger, - *pedestrian*
die Haltestelle, -n *bus stop, train stop*
das Licht, -er *light*
die S-Bahn (Stadtbahn), -en *subway that travels outside the city above ground*
das Schild, -er *sign*

das Transportmittel, - *means of transportation*
die U-Bahn (Untergrundbahn), -en *subway*
die Verkehrsampel, -n *traffic light*

halten (hält), hielt, gehalten *to stop*

Einfahrt verboten! *Do not enter!*
die Straße überqueren *to cross the street*

ZUM BESPRECHEN

1. Beschreiben Sie das Bild.
2. Darf man die Straße überqueren? Woher wissen Sie das (sehen Sie sich auch das nächste Foto an!)?
3. Wo hält der Bus? Woher wissen Sie, daß der Bus hier hält?
4. Welche anderen Transportmittel gibt es in der Nähe? Woher wissen Sie das?
5. Woher weiß man, daß die Straße eine Einbahnstraße ist?

An der Kreuzung

WORTSCHATZ

der Bahnhof, ⸚e *railroad station*
das Gebäude, - *building*
die Hochschule, -n *university*
die Kathedrale, -n *cathedral*
die Kreuzung, -en *crossing*
das Land, ⸚er *country*
das Paar, -e *pair*
die Richtung, -en *direction*
die Stiftsbibliothek *monastery library*
  (St. Gallen, Switzerland)

der Zebrastreifen *stripes (on a crossing)*

besprechen (bespricht), besprach, besprochen *to discuss*
erreichen *to reach*
stammen aus *to come from, originate*

links *left*
rechts *right*
verschieden *various*

42

ZUM BESPRECHEN

1. Beschreiben Sie die Szene auf Seite 42.
2. Worüber spricht das Paar, das die Straße überquert?
3. Aus welchem Land stammt dieses Foto? Woher wissen Sie das?
4. Welche Plätze und Städte kann man von dieser Kreuzung aus erreichen? In welche Richtungen muß man gehen oder fahren, um diese Gebäude und Städte zu erreichen?
5. Warum sollte der Fußgänger die Straße nur am Zebrastreifen überqueren?

Am Marktplatz 1.

2.

WORTSCHATZ

der Apfel, ⸚ *apple*
der Arm, -e *arm*
die Banane, -n *banana*
der Besitzer, - *owner*
die Einkaufstasche, -n *shopping bag*
die Erdbeere, -n *strawberry*
die Gurke, -n *cucumber*
das Kilo (gramm) *kilogram (= 2.2 pounds)*
der Marktplatz, ⸚e *market-place*
das Obst, -sorten *fruit*

der Pfirsich, -e *peach*
der Stand, ⸚e *stand*
das Stück, -e *piece*
die Tomate, -n *tomato*
die Traube, -n *grape*
die Tüte, -n *bag*
die Waage, -n *scale*

brauchen *to need*
wiegen, wog, gewogen *to weigh*

43

ZUM BESPRECHEN

1. Beschreiben Sie die Szene auf dem Foto Nr. 1 (Seite 43) so vollständig wie möglich.
2. Was für Obstsorten sehen Sie auf dem Foto Nr. 2? Welches Obst hätten Sie gerne?
3. Wieviel kosten zwei Kilo Äpfel? Wieviel kostet ein Apfel? (Foto 1)
4. Was trägt die Kundin am Arm? Wofür braucht sie das?
5. Gibt es in Ihrer Stadt auch solche Marktplätze, wo Sie Obst einkaufen können?

Der Polizist

WORTSCHATZ

der Handschuh, -e *glove*
der Hut, ⸚e *hat*
der Polizist, -en, -en *policeman*
das Sprechfunkgerät, -e *walkie-talkie*
der Umstand, ⸚e *circumstance*

die Uniform, -en *uniform*
der Vorgang, ⸚e *incident, event*

schildern *to describe, portray*

ZUM BESPRECHEN

1. Schildern Sie die Vorgänge in dieser Szene und wie es dazu gekommen ist. Benutzen Sie Ihre Phantasie dabei.
2. Welche Pflichten hat ein Polizist in der Stadt?
3. Beschreiben Sie die Uniform des Polizisten.
4. Beschreiben Sie die Umstände, unter denen Sie das letzte Mal mit einem Polizisten gesprochen haben.

44

Am Kiosk

WORTSCHATZ

die Ansichtskarte, -n *picture postcard*
der Führerschein, -e *driver's license*
die Illustrierte, -n *illustrated magazine*
der Inhalt *contents*
der Kiosk, -e *newsstand*
die Zeitkarte, -n *season ticket*

die Zeitschrift, -en *magazine*
die Zeitung, -en *newspaper*

fordern *to demand*

auf Lebenseit *for life*
Zeitung lesen *to read the newspaper*

ZUM BESPRECHEN

1. Welche Zeitungen kann man an diesem Kiosk kaufen?
2. Was kann man außer Zeitungen noch kaufen?
3. Was macht der junge Mann, der vor dem Kiosk steht?
4. Lesen Sie jeden Tag Zeitung? Warum oder warum nicht?
5. Welche Zeitschriften kaufen Sie jeden Monat? Beschreiben Sie den Inhalt jeder der Zeitschriften.
6. Beschreiben Sie den Unterschied zwischen einer Zeitschrift und einer Zeitung.

45

Deutsche Geschäfte und das Postamt

Das Einkaufszentrum

WORTSCHATZ

das Einkaufszentrum, -tren *shopping center*

die Fußgängerzone, -n *pedestrian zone, mall*

das Geschäft, -e, der Laden, ¨ *store, shop*

Andre: das Schuhgeschäft, -e *shoe store*

Commerzbank: die Bank, -en *bank*

Dugena: die Damenboutique, -en *women's boutique*

Kämpgen: das Fotogeschäft, -e *photo store*

Kettner: das Spielwarengeschäft, -e *toy store*

Langhardt: das Lederwarengeschäft, -e *leather goods store*

Michiko, da Vinci: das Schmuckwarengeschäft, -e *jewelry store*

Wormland: das Herrengeschäft, -e *men's store*

einen Stadtbummel machen *to take a stroll through the city*

einkaufen gehen *to go shopping*

Geld ab·heben, hob ab, abgehoben *to withdraw money*

ZUM BESPRECHEN

1. Welche Vorteile hat eine Fußgängerzone?
2. Wieso ist es vorteilhaft a) eine Bank b) ein Restaurant/Café im Einkaufszentrum zu haben?
3. Machen Sie mit Ihrem Partner einen Stadtbummel durch das Einkaufszentrum in Köln (siehe Foto oben!). Kaufen Sie in jedem Laden etwas ein! Geld spielt natürlich keine Rolle.

Inter Discount	Photo, Radio, Hi-Fi
Ladenchef:	GOERTZ HENRY
Ladenöffnungszeiten	
Montag	GESCHLOSSEN
Dienstag	9.00 – 12 / 13 – 18.30
Mittwoch	9.00 – 12 / 13 – 18.30
Donnerstag	9.00 – 12 / 13 – 18.30
Freitag	9.00 – 12 / 13 – 18.30
Samstag	9.00 – 12 / 13 – 17.00
Unsere Tel. Nr. [071]	23 23 20

Das Geschäft

WORTSCHATZ

der Discount-Laden, ⸚ *discount store*
das Hi-Fi Gerät, -e *hi-fi equipment*
die Kamera, -s, Fotoapparat, -e
   camera
der Ladenchef, -s *shop manager*
die Öffnungszeiten *store hours*
das Radio, -s *radio*

die Sache, -n *thing, article*
die Stereoanlage, -n *stereo system*
die Telefonnummer, -n *telephone*
   number

schließen, schloß, geschlossen *to*
   close

ZUM BESPRECHEN

1. Welche Sachen kann man in dem „Inter Discount" Laden kaufen?
2. Inwiefern unterscheiden sich die Ladenöffnungszeiten im „Inter Discount" von denen in Ihrer Stadt?
3. Wie heißt der Ladenchef?
4. Was macht der Ladenchef zwischen 12 und 13 Uhr?
5. Warum steht auch die Telefonnummer auf dem Schild?
6. Kaufen Sie oft Sachen in einem Discounthaus? Warum oder warum nicht?

47

Das Reisebüro

WORTSCHATZ

der Anfänger, - *beginner*
das Angebot, -e *offer*
der Flug, ⸚e *flight*
der Hinflug, ⸚e *flight to a destination*
der Kurs, -e *course*
das Olympiabad *Olympic pool*
  (Munich)

die Reise, -n *trip*
das Reisebüro, -s *travel bureau*
der Rückflug, -e *return flight*

fliegen, flog, ist geflogen *to fly*
planen *to plan*
tauchen *to dive*

ZUM BESPRECHEN

Besprechen Sie die Flugangebote auf dem Foto mit einem Kommilitonen in der Klasse. Planen Sie dann eine Reise mit ihm oder ihr!

Die Herrenboutique

Das Brillengeschäft

WORTSCHATZ

der Anzug, ⸚e *suit*
das Brillengeschäft, -e *optician*
der Gürtel, - *belt*
das Hemd, -en *shirt*
die Herrenboutique, -en *men's boutique*
die Hose, -n *trousers (eine Hose = one pair of trousers)*
die Jacke, -n, der Sakko, -s *sport jacket*
die Jeans, - *jeans*
die Kleidung *clothing*

die Kontaktlinse, -n *contact lens*
die Krawatte, -n, der Schlips, -e *tie*
die Mode, -n *fashion*
der Pullover, - *sweater*
der Schuh, -e *shoe*

aus·suchen *to pick out*
tragen (trägt), trug, getragen *to wear to carry*
eine Brille tragen *to wear glasses*

49

ZUM BESPRECHEN

1. Was macht der Herr auf dem Foto in der Herrenboutique? Woran denkt er wahrscheinlich?
2. Beschreiben Sie die Kleidung, die Sie tragen:
   - a) in der Schule
   - b) zu Hause
   - c) zur Kirche
   - d) zum Skilaufen
   - e) zum formellen Abendessen
3. Würden Sie lieber eine Brille oder Kontaktlinsen tragen? Warum?

Andere Läden

Die Apotheke

ZUM BESPRECHEN _____

    1. Braucht man für alles, was man in einer Apotheke kauft, ein Rezept?
    2. Welche Stress-Situation in der „Aktren" Reklame bereitet Ihnen die größten Kopfschmerzen?

Die Reinigung

ZUM BESPRECHEN _____

    1. Warum heißt diese Reinigung „Quick"?
    2. Welche Kleider bringen Sie normalerweise zu einer Reinigung? Welche bringen Sie normalerweise *nicht* dahin?

Die Buchhandlung

ZUM BESPRECHEN

1. Was für Bücher lesen Sie gerne? Lesen Sie lieber Romane oder Sachbücher?
2. Beschreiben Sie Ihrem Kommilitonen in der Klasse Ihr Lieblingsbuch.
3. Sehen Sie sich das Bild von den Büchern an. Welche drei Frauen sind Ihrer Meinung nach die berühmtesten der Weltgeschichte? Begründen Sie Ihre Antwort! Welche drei Männer sind die berühmtesten der Weltgeschichte?
4. Nennen Sie einige Märchen der Gebrüder Grimm. Können Sie eines davon nacherzählen?
5. Stellen Sie sich vor, Sie hätten ein Buch geschrieben. Sprechen Sie über dessen Inhalt! Gebrauchen Sie viel Phantasie dabei!

Die Bäckerei/die Konditorei

ZUM BESPRECHEN

1. Was macht die Verkäuferin hinter dem Fenster (Seite 52)?
2. Was kaufen Sie gerne in einer Bäckerei?

Das Kino

ZUM BESPRECHEN

1. Welcher Film läuft in diesem Kino?
2. Um wieviel Uhr beginnen die Filmvorstellungen in diesem Kino?
3. Wie unterscheiden sich die Preise von Kinoplätzen in Deutschland von denen in Amerika?
4. Beschreiben Sie Ihrem Partner in der Klasse den letzten Film, den Sie gesehen haben.
5. Beschreiben Sie Ihren Lieblingsfilm!

Auf dem Postamt

WORTSCHATZ

die Angabe, -n   *statement*
der Briefkasten, ⸚   *mail box*
das Paket, -e   *package, parcel*
das Postamt, ⸚er   *post office*

schleppen   *to pull, drag*

auf dem Postamt   *at the post office*
einen Brief, ein Paket auf·geben,
  ab·senden   *to mail a letter, a*
  package
einen Brief ein·werfen   *to drop a letter*
  in a mailbox

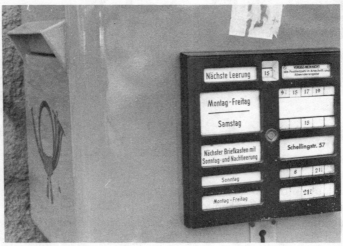

der Briefkasten

ZUM BESPRECHEN

1. Beschreiben Sie die Szene auf diesem Bild (Seite 54 oben).
2. Wie oft wird dieser Briefkasten (Seite 54 unten) geleert?
3. Wann ist die nächste Leerung?
4. Warum ist der Standort des nächsten Briefkastens in der Schellingstraße angegeben?
5. Welche Informationen findet man auf einem deutschen Briefkasten im Gegensatz zu einem amerikanischen?

POSTGEBÜHREN

Standardbrief (Inland)	DM 0,50
Postkarte (Inland)	DM 0,40
Standardbrief (Ausland)	DM 0,70
Postkarte (Ausland)	DM 0,50
Luftpostbrief bis 5 g	DM 0,90
Einschreibegebühr	DM 1,40

WORTSCHATZ

das Ausland *foreign country, abroad*
der Brief, -e *letter*
die Briefmarke, -n *stamp*
das Gramm *gram (= 0.035 ounces)*
das Inland *native country, domestic*
die Post *mail; post office*
die Postgebühr, -en *postal fee*

die Postkarte, -n *postcard*
die Postleitzahl, -en *zip code*
der Poststempel, - *postmark*

einen Brief einschreiben lassen *to register a letter*
per Luftpost *by air mail*

ZUM BESPRECHEN

1. Kostet ein Brief in Deutschland mehr oder weniger als in Amerika? (1 DM = ungefähr 50¢)
2. Wieviel kostet ein Brief von Frankfurt nach Zürich? Eine Postkarte von Hamburg nach Stuttgart? Ein Luftpostbrief von Deutschland nach Michigan?
3. Wann läßt man einen Brief einschreiben?
4. Kaufen Sie auf dem Postamt Briefmarken für Ihre Briefe und Päckchen. Spielen Sie mit einem Kommilitonen die Rollen von Kunden und Postbeamten. Stellen Sie so viele Fragen wie möglich.
5. Was kann man alles aus dem Poststempel ablesen?

55

DAS HOTEL

6

WORTSCHATZ

das Appartement, -s   *suite of rooms, efficiency apartment*
das Bad, ⸚er   *bath*
das Doppelzimmer, -   *double room*
die Dusche, -n   *shower*
das Einbettzimmer, -   *single room*
die Eltern (*pl.*)   *parents*
die Entspannung   *relaxation*
das Extrabett, -en   *extra bed*
das Fernsehen   *TV*
der Fitnessraum, ⸚e   *fitness room*
die Garage, -n   *garage*
der Hauptbahnhof, ⸚e   *main railway station*
das Hotel, -s   *hotel*
der Inklusivpreis, -e   *inclusive price*
die Klimaanlage, -n   *air conditioning*
der Komfort   *luxury*
die Lage, -n   *location, situation*
die Massage   *massage*
der Pensionspreis, -e   *pension, boarding-house price*
das Radio, -s   *radio*
die Ruhe   *rest*
die Ruhezone, -n   *rest area*
die Sauna, -s   *sauna*
das Schwimmbad, ⸚er   *swimming pool*
die Sonnenterrasse, -n   *sun terrace*

das Telefon, -e   *telephone*
die Unterbringung   *accommodation*
die Vereinbarung, -en   *agreement, arrangement*
das WC, -s (das Wasserklosett, -s)   *toilet, washroom*
die Zentralheizung, -en   *central heating*
das Zimmer, -   *room*

bieten, bot, geboten   *to offer*
ein·schließen, schloß ein, eingeschlossen   *to include*
enthalten (enthält), enthielt, enthalten   *to include, contain*
übernachten   *to stay overnight*

ausgestattet   *equipped*
einschließlich   *inclusive*
erstklassig   *first-class*
großräumig   *spacious*
vorbildlich   *ideal(ly)*
willkommen   *welcome*
zweitklassig   *second-class*

fließendes Wasser   *running water*
in nächster Nähe   *very nearby*

57

ZUM BESPRECHEN

1. Welches Hotel ist ein erstklassiges Hotel? Ein zweitklassiges Hotel?
2. In welchem Hotel möchten Sie übernachten? Warum?
3. Ist das Frühstück in beiden Hotels im Zimmerpreis eingeschlossen? Begründen Sie Ihre Antwort!
4. Erklären Sie den Unterschied zwischen den Einzelzimmern zu DM 26,-, DM 34,-, und DM 45,- im Hotel Haberstock.
5. Müssen die Eltern extra bezahlen, wenn sie ihre beiden Kinder ins Hotel Vier Jahreszeiten mitbringen?

ZUR AUSFÜHRLICHEN DISKUSSION

1. Beschreiben Sie eine Nacht, die Sie in einem Hotel verbracht haben.
2. Beschreiben Sie ein Hotelzimmer, in dem Sie übernachtet haben.

Ein Straßenplan Münchens

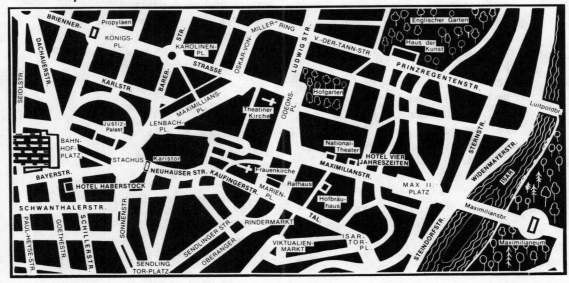

Auf der Straße in München

PAUL: Entschuldigen Sie, Herr Wachtmeister. Können Sie mir sagen, wo das Hotel Haberstock ist?

DER POLIZIST: Ja. In der Schillerstraße in der Nähe vom Bahnhof.

PAUL: Ist es sehr weit von hier?

DER POLIZIST: Nein, nicht weit. Sie können zu Fuß gehen. Es ist ungefähr fünf Minuten von hier.

PAUL: Können Sie mir den Weg zeigen?

DER POLIZIST: Gern. Wir sind jetzt am Stachus.* Gehen Sie die Bayerstraße hinunter und dann links um die Ecke. Dann sehen Sie das Hotel Haberstock gegenüber einem Filmtheater.

PAUL: Muß ich am Bahnhofplatz vorbeigehen?

DER POLIZIST: Nein. Der Bahnhofplatz liegt rechts. Sie gehen links um die Ecke.

PAUL: Also, danke schön, Herr Wachtmeister!

DER POLIZIST: Bitte schön!

WORTSCHATZ

das Hofbräuhaus *Hofbräuhaus*
die Kirche, -n *church*
der Palast, ⸚e *palace*
der Platz, ⸚e *place, square*
der Polizist, -en *policeman*
der Stadtplan, ⸚e *city map*
das Theater, - *theater*
der Wachtmeister, - *police officer*

entschuldigen *to excuse*
vorbei·gehen, ging vorbei, ist vorbeigegangen an (+ *dat.*) *to go past, go by*
vor·haben *to plan*

nah *near*
ungefähr *approximately*
weit *far*

auf der Straße *on the street*
bitte schön *you're welcome*
den Weg zeigen *to give directions*
günstig gelegen *to be favorably situated or located*
in der Schillerstraße *on Schiller Street*
zu Fuß gehen *to walk, go by foot*

ZUM BESPRECHEN

1. Suchen Sie sich einen Partner in der Klasse, und sehen Sie sich den Straßenplan Münchens an. Sie sind am Bahnhof in München. Fragen Sie Ihren Partner, wie Sie zum Hotel Vier Jahreszeiten kommen.
2. Wählen Sie einen anderen Partner. Jetzt sind Sie im Hofbräuhaus. Fragen Sie Ihren Partner nach dem Weg zum Hotel Haberstock.
3. Sie haben vor, einen Tag in München zu verbringen. Welches Hotel ist für Sie am günstigsten gelegen? Warum?

59

---

* Einkaufszentrum in München

Im Hotel Haberstock

WORTSCHATZ

das Anmeldeformular, -e *registration form*
der Gast, ⸚e *guest*
das Gepäck *luggage*
der Kalender, - *calendar*
der Portier, -s *porter*
der Prospekt, -e *prospectus*
der Schlüssel, - *key*
die Szene, -n *scene*
der Wirt, -e *innkeeper (male)*
die Wirtin, -nen *innkeeper (female)*

sich ab·melden *to check out*
an·bieten, bot an, angeboten *to offer*
sich an·melden *to check in, register*
sich beklagen bei jemandem über etwas
  (acc.) *to complain to someone about something*

ein Bild, Foto aufnehmen *to take a picture*
in Ordnung *in order*

ZUM BESPRECHEN

1. Glauben Sie, daß die Bilder (Seite 60) im Hotel Haberstock oder im Hotel Vier Jahreszeiten aufgenommen sind? Begründen Sie Ihre Antwort.
2. Was macht die Dame auf dem Foto oben?
3. Was tut der Gast auf dem Foto unten? Was schreibt man auf ein Anmeldeformular?
4. Das Hotel bietet viele Prospekte an. Welche Informationen kann der Gast darin finden?
5. Welcher Tag ist es? Woher wissen Sie das?
6. Wieviel wird der Gast für sein Einzelzimmer zahlen müssen, wenn er bis zum sechzehnten bleibt?

ZUR AUSFÜHRLICHEN DISKUSSION

1. Spielen Sie die Rollen von Wirt(in) und Gast. Fragen Sie so viel wie möglich über das Hotel und die Preise.
2. Sie finden, daß Ihr Hotelzimmer nicht in Ordnung ist. Beklagen Sie sich bei der Wirtin darüber.

61

DIE FAMILIE

7

Im Wohnzimmer

WORTSCHATZ

das Bild, -er *picture, photograph*
der Boden, ⸚ *floor*
der Bruder, ⸚ *brother*
der Couchtisch, -e *coffee table*
die Familie, -n *family*
das Familienmitglied, -er *family member*

der Fernsehapparat, -e *TV set*
die Frau, -en *woman, wife*
der Gegenstand, ⸚e *object*
die Geschwister (*pl.*) *brothers and sisters*
der Globus, -se *globe*
die Großmutter, ⸚ *grandmother*

der Großvater, ∺ *grandfather*
das Hobby, -s *hobby*
der Jäger, - *hunter*
der Kronleuchter, - *chandelier*
der Mann, ∺er *husband, man*
das Möbelstück, -e *piece of furniture*
die Mutter, ∺ *mother*
der Onkel, - *uncle*
die Pflanze, -n *plant*
der Schrank, ∺e *closet, wall unit*
die Schwester, -n *sister*
der Sessel, - *armchair*
das Sofa, -s *sofa*
der Sohn, ∺e *son*
die Tante, -n *aunt*
der Teppich, -e *rug, carpet*

die Tochter, ∺ *daughter*
der Vater, ∺ *father*
der/die Verwandte, -n *relative*

besprechen, besprach, besprochen *to discuss*
fern·sehen (sieht fern), sah fern, ferngesehen *to watch TV*
jagen *to hunt*
zu·hören (+ *dat.*) *to listen to*

ausführlich *in detail, fully*
sich beschäftigen mit (+ *dat.*) to be *busy with*
sich eine Fernsehsendung anschauen *to watch a TV program*

ZUM BESPRECHEN

1. Welche Familienmitglieder sehen Sie auf dem Bild? Was machen sie?
2. Welche Möbelstücke und welche anderen Gegenstände sehen Sie im Wohnzimmer?
3. Worüber unterhalten sich die Frauen wahrscheinlich?
4. Womit beschäftigt sich der Vater? Warum spricht er nicht mit den Damen?
5. Wo steht der Schrank? Wo steht der Fernsehapparat? Der Globus?
6. Was für ein Hobby hat der Vater? Woher wissen Sie das?

ZUR AUSFÜHRLICHEN DISKUSSION

1. Wie unterscheidet sich dieses deutsche Wohnzimmer von Ihrem Wohnzimmer zu Hause?
2. Beschreiben Sie einem Klassenkameraden so ausführlich wie möglich, Ihre Familie und Ihre Verwandten. Vergessen Sie dabei die Hunde und Katzen nicht!
3. Beschreiben Sie eines Ihrer Hobbies.

63

Freitag, 25. Februar
2. Programm

das Programm, -e = *program for the day, channel*

16.30 Turn mit
Noch einmal Obungen mit dem Reifen und Ball

turnen = *to do gymnastics*
die Übung = *exercise*
der Reifen = *tire*

17.00 Das internationale Tanztheater
Romeo und Julia (Wh)
Ballett nach Shakespeare und Sergei Prokofieff in der Choreographie von John Cranko. Es tanzt das Ballett des Württembergischen Staatstheaters

17.40 Tanzparty
18.20 Dick und Doof
Selige Campingfreuden
Mit Stan Laurel und Oliver Hardy

selig = *blissful*

19.00 Heute
19.30 Die Waltons
20.15 Du
Von Christian Doermer
(Für Jugendliche nicht geeignet)

die Tagesschau = *"news and views"*

Wim G. arbeitet in einer Investitionsbank in Bangkok. Freunde helfen ihm bei der Einrichtung der Wohnung und vermitteln ihm eine Hausangestellte. Das Mädchen spricht nur Thai. Weil sich Wim G. den Namen nicht merken kann, nennt er das Mädchen einfach „Du". Er bemüht sich, ihr Deutsch beizubringen und lernt selber Thai. Bald kommt es zu einem „eheähnlichen" Verhältnis zwischen den beiden. Als sie gemeinsam Urlaub in Europa machen, gibt es erste Schwierigkeiten . . . Foto: Suwanit Wirodjanawat, Christian Doermer, Lore Peterson

21.15 Kennen Sie Kino?
Fernsehquiz fur Kinogänger
Mit Hellmut Lange

die Freude = *joy*
der/die Jugendliche = *young people*
geeignet = *suitable*
die Einrichtung = *arrangement, furnishing*
vermitteln (+ dat.) = *to secure for;*
die Hausangestellte = *housemaid*
sich merken = *to remember*
sich bemühen = *to try, endeavor*
bei·bringen (+ dat.) = *to teach*
eheähnlich = *quasi-marital*
das Verhältnis = *relationship*
der Urlaub = *vacation*
die Schwierigkeit = *difficulty*
der Kinogänger = *movie-goer*
auf der Suche nach = *in search of*

21.30 Auf der Suche nach der Welt von morgen NDR
Die Herausforderung der Menschheit (1). Die Explosion der Weltbevölkerung. Von Rüdiger Proske

die Herausforderung = *challenge*
die Bevölkerung = *population*

22.15 Sport am Freitag
Endrundenspiele der Eishockey-Bundesliga

das Endrundenspiel = *playoff*

22.45 Treck nach Utah
Amerikanischer Spielfilm von 1940

Die von Joseph Smith gegründete Religionsgemeinschaft der Mormonen wird im Osten der USA seit Jahren verfolgt. Die Mormonen ziehen nach Illinois und geben dort ihr Prinzip der Gewaltlosigkeit auf. Smith wird 1844 vor Gericht gestellt, zum Tode verurteilt, vor der Hinrichtung aber gelyncht. Daraufhin ziehen die Mormonen in einem Treck nach Utah . . . Foto: Tyrone Power, Linda Darnell. Regie: H. Hathaway

gründen = *to found*
die Gemeinschaft = *community*
verfolgen = *to pursue, persecute*
ziehen nach = *to move to;*
auf·geben (gibt auf), gab auf, aufgegeben = *to give up*
das Gericht, -e = *court* zum Tode verurteilt = *sentenced to death*
die Hinrichtung, -en = *execution*

ZUM BESPRECHEN

1. Woran bemerken Sie den Einfluß Amerikas auf das deutsche Fernsehen?
2. Welche Sendungen im 2. Programm würden Sie sich gerne anschauen? Warum?
3. Wie heißen ,,Dick und Doof" auf englisch?
4. Erzählen Sie kurz die Geschichte von Romeo und Julia nach!
5. Wovon handelt der Fernsehfilm ,,Du"? Warum heißt das Mädchen ,,Du"? Warum ist der Film ,,nicht für Jugendliche geeignet"?
6. Worüber spricht man in der Sendung ,,Auf der Suche nach der Welt von morgen"?
7. Wovon handelt der Spielfilm ,,Treck nach Utah"?
8. Wie unterscheidet sich das deutsche Fernsehen vom amerikanischen Fernsehen? Schauen Sie sich besonders die Vormittagssendungen an!

ZUR AUSFÜHRLICHEN DISKUSSION

1. Was kann man abends alles tun, wenn man nicht fernsieht?
2. Beschreiben Sie Ihrem Kollegen Ihre Lieblingssendung im Fernsehen.
3. Glauben Sie, daß man heutzutage zu viel fernsieht? Nennen Sie einige Vor- und Nachteile des Fernsehens.

65

Am Eßtisch

WORTSCHATZ

das Essen, - *meal*
der Eßtisch, -e *dining room table*
das Fleisch *meat*
die Gabel, -n *fork*
das Gericht, -e *dish, course*
das Glas, ¨er *glass*
die Kerze, -n *candle*
der Knödel, - *dumpling*
der Löffel, - *spoon*
die Mahlzeit, -en *meal, mealtime*
das Messer, - *knife*
der Nachtisch, -e *dessert*
der Salat, -e *salad*
die Serviette, -n *napkin*
die Soßenschüssel, -n *gravy dish*
die Stehlampe, -n *floor lamp*
die Vorspeise, -n *appetizer*
der Teller, - *plate*

an·fangen (fängt an), fing an,
  angefangen *to start, begin*
aus·sehen (sieht aus), sah aus,
  ausgesehen (wie) *to look (like),
  appear*
servieren *to serve*

alltäglich *everyday*
festlich *festive*
gekleidet *dressed*
hungrig *hungry*
satt *satisfied, full*
zuletzt *finally, in the end*

dabei sein *to be there*
denken an (+acc.) *to think of*
den Tisch decken *to set the table*
greifen nach (+dat.) *to reach for*

66 ZUM BESPRECHEN

1. Was hat die Mutter in der Hand? Was tut Sie damit?
2. Was macht der Junge?
3. Was denkt seine Schwester wahrscheinlich?

4. Woher wissen Sie, daß ein deutsches Essen serviert wird?
5. Stellt das Bild den Anfang oder das Ende der Mahlzeit dar? Warum?
6. Glauben Sie, daß dies ein alltägliches oder ein festliches Essen ist?

ZUR AUSFÜHRLICHEN DISKUSSION

1. Beschreiben Sie ein alltägliches Abendessen bei sich zu Hause. Wer kocht? Mit welchem Gericht fangen Sie an? Was essen Sie zuletzt?
2. Wie oft gibt es ein festliches Essen bei Ihnen zu Hause? Wer ist normalerweise dabei? Welche Gerichte werden serviert?
3. Beschreiben Sie, wie man einen Tisch deckt.

Die Zubereitung des Essens

WORTSCHATZ

das Bord, -e *shelf, board*
der Essig *vinegar*
das Gewürz, -e *spice, seasoning*
das Kästchen, - *small chest*
der Kühlschrank, ⸚e *refrigerator*
das Öl *oil*
der Pfeffer *pepper*
das Salz *salt*
die Schüssel, -n *bowl*
die Zubereitung, -en *preparation*

lächeln *to smile*
probieren *to try out, test, taste*
zu·bereiten *to prepare*

hinterher *afterwards*
wohl *probably*

einen Salat an·machen *to prepare a salad*
gut oder nicht gut schmecken *to taste good or bad*

67

ZUM BESPRECHEN

1. In welchem Raum spielt die Szene auf Seite 67?
2. Was macht die Mutter? Warum lächelt sie?
3. Was macht die Tochter? Was wird sie wohl hinterher sagen?
4. Was steht wahrscheinlich in dem Kästchen an der Wand?
5. Welchen Unterschied sehen Sie zwischen einem deutschen und einem amerikanischen Kühlschrank?
6. Beschreiben Sie Ihr Lieblingsessen und wie man es zubereitet.

WIENER KIRSCHTORTE (12 Stück, 305 Kalorien pro Stück)

Zutaten:

140 g Margarine	*margarine (1 g = 0.035 ounces)*
140 g Zucker	*sugar*
3 Eigelb	*egg yolks*
1 Prise Zimt	*pinch of cinnamon*
1 Teelöffel Rum	*rum*
Zitronenschale	*lemon peel*
100 g Mehl	*flour*
2 gestrichene Teelöffel Backpulver	*level teaspoons baking powder*
50 g gemahlene Mandeln	*crushed almonds*
3 Eiweiß	*egg whites*
500 g entkernte Kirschen	*pitted cherries*
Puderzucker	*powdered sugar*
¼ Liter geschlagene Sahne	*whipped cream (1 Liter = 1.057 quarts)*

Rezept:

Weiches Fett in eine hohe Schüssel geben. Zucker, Eigelb, Zimt, Rum, Zitronenschale und das mit Backpulver gemischte Mehl dazugeben. Alles mit dem Handrührgerät auf höchster Schaltstufe verrühren. Gemahlene Mandeln dazugeben und zuletzt das steifgeschlagene Eiweiß unterheben. Den Teig in eine gefettete Springform füllen und mit entsteinten Kirschen belegen. Im vorgeheizten Backofen backen. Die erkaltete Kirschtorte mit Puderzucker bestäuben und mit Sahne servieren. Backzeit: 60 Minuten Herd: 180 – 200° C

weich = soft
gemischt = mixed
das Handrührgerät = hand mixer
die höchste Schaltstufe = set on
    „high"; verrühren = to mix
steif = stiff/unter·heben, hob
    unter, untergehoben = to fold
    in; der Teig = dough
die Springform = spring form pan
belegen = to cover/vorgeheizt =
    pre-heated
bestäuben = to sprinkle

$(= 350 - 400° F) (F = \frac{18C}{10} + 32)$

68

ZUM BESPRECHEN

1. Bringen Sie Ihr Lieblingsrezept in die Klasse mit und beschreiben Sie es Ihren Kommilitonen.
2. Backen Sie eine Wiener Kirschtorte für die Klasse!
3. Welches Argument spricht a) für selbstgebackenen Kuchen b) gegen selbstgebackenen Kuchen?
4. Männer in der Küche: besprechen Sie das Für und Wider!
5. Was verstehen Sie unter dem Satz ,,Viele Köche verderben den Brei''?

Das Zimmer eines Teenagers

WORTSCHATZ

das Bücherregal, -e *book-shelf*
der Filmstar, -s *film star*
die Puppe, -n *doll*
der Rockstar, -s *rock star*
der Sänger, - *singer*

die Schallplatte, -n *record*
der Teenager, - *teenager*

dar·stellen *to depict*
erkennen, erkannte, erkannt *to recognize*

69

ZUM BESPRECHEN

1. Worüber könnten die Geschwister auf dem Bild (Seite 69) sprechen?
2. Stellt dieses Bild ein Mädchenzimmer oder ein Jungenzimmer dar? Woher wissen Sie das?
3. Was für Bilder sehen Sie an der Wand?
4. Beschreiben Sie Ihr eigenes Zimmer zu Hause.
5. Wer ist Ihr Lieblingsfilmstar? Ihr Lieblingssänger oder Ihre Lieblingssängerin? Erklären Sie das näher!

Das Picknick

WORTSCHATZ

der Garten, ⸚ *garden, yard*
der Korb, ⸚e *basket*
das Picknick, -s *picnic*
das Sandwich, -es; das belegte Brot, -e *sandwich*

aus·wählen *to choose*
fressen (frißt), fraß, gefressen *to eat (of animals)*
statt·finden, fand statt, stattgefunden *to take place*

70

ZUM BESPRECHEN

1. Beschreiben Sie das Foto.
2. Was sagt wohl der Vater auf dem Bild?
3. Was „denkt" der Hund wahrscheinlich?
4. Was bringt man normalerweise zu einem Picknick mit?
5. Wie wählt man einen guten Picknickplatz aus?
6. Beschreiben Sie Ihren Klassenkameraden ein Picknick, das Sie mit Ihrer Familie oder Ihren Freunden gemacht haben.

SCHULE UND BERUF

8

Eine der wichtigsten Grundlagen für die Berufswahl ist die Schule, also der Schulabschluß: es gibt die Hauptschule mit dem Hauptschulabschluß, die Realschule mit der ,,Mittleren Reife" und das Gymnasium mit dem Abitur. Wer sich entschließt, Handwerker oder Facharbeiter zu werden, muß nach dem Besuch der Hauptschule eine dreijährige Berufsausbildung machen.

Die ,,Mittlere Reife" berechtigt einen, eine Fachschule zu besuchen. Einige Beispiele: der Techniker für elektronische Rechengeräte, der Programmierer, oder der Kaufmann; auch die MTA (Medizinisch-Technische-Assistentin) gehört in diesen Bereich, ebenso wie der Sozialarbeiter oder der Optiker.

Das Abitur berechtigt jeden, eine Hochschule oder eine Universität zu besuchen. Aus dem Schüler wird ein Student, der mindestens vier Jahre studieren muß, um einen Beruf zu erlangen. Wer z.B. Arzt, Lehrer, Richter oder Wissenschaftler werden will, muß eine Universität besuchen. Nach dem Studium kann jeder selber entscheiden, ob er selbständig arbeiten oder sich von einer Firma oder einer Behörde anstellen lassen will. Er wird dann Angestellter oder Beamter und erhält für seine Arbeit einen Monatsgehalt. Arbeiter sind keine Angestellten, sie erhalten einen Wochenlohn. Will jemand Selbstständiger sein, zum Beispiel als Architekt, so kann er allein oder mit anderen ein Architektenbüro gründen. Ein Arzt kann eine eigene Praxis führen.

Früher gab es weniger Berufe als heute. Mit der Entwicklung der Technik wurden besonders in unserem Jahrhundert auch neue Berufe geschaffen: beispielsweise Radio-und Fernsehmechaniker, Elektriker oder Autotechniker.

72

Heute gibt es in der Bundesrepublik Deutschland über 20,000 verschiedene Berufe. Deshalb ist es für den einzelnen sehr schwer, den für ihn richtigen Beruf zu finden. Um diese Suche etwas zu erleichtern, haben die Arbeitsämter Berufsberatungsstellen eingerichtet. Hier kann jeder genaue Auskunft über alle Berufsmöglichkeiten erhalten.

Berufslaufbahnen

I. Landwirt, Maler, Friseur, Koch, Automechaniker, Fabrikarbeiter, Maurer, Tischler, Schneider, Schuster, Beamter (Polizist, Lokomotivführer, Briefträger), Verkäufer(in), usw.

Alter:

6 – 15	Hauptschule (Abschluß: Hauptschulabschluß)
15 – 18	Lehrjahre und Berufsschule (einmal in der Woche) (Abschluß: Gesellenprüfung)

II. Techniker, Programmierer, Sekretärin, Sozialarbeiter, Kaufmann, technische Berufe (Chemotechniker, MTA, Krankenschwester), Optiker, usw.

Alter:

6 – 10	Hauptschule
10 – 16	Realschule (Abschluß: ,, Mittlere Reife'')
16 – 18	Fachschule oder Firma

III. Wissenschaftliche/akademische Berufe: Arzt, Lehrer, Rechtsanwalt, Richter, Ingenieur, Wissenschaftler, usw.

Alter:

6 – 10	Hauptschule
10 – 19	Gymnasium (Abschluß: Abitur)
19 – 24	Universität oder Hochschule (Abschluß: Staatsexamen oder Diplom)

WORTSCHATZ

das Abitur   *diploma from German "Gymnasium"*

der Abschluß, ̈sse   *diploma*

der Angestellte, -n, -n (ein Angestellter)   *employee (salaried)*

das Arbeitsamt, ̈er   *employment agency*

der Architekt, -en, -en   *architect*

der Arzt, ̈e   *physician*

die Auskunft, ̈e   *information*

der Beamte, -n, -n (ein Beamter)   *official, civil servant*

die Behörde, -n   *(local) government*

der Beruf, -e   *profession*

die Berufsausbildung, -en   *education for a profession*

die Berufsberatungsstelle, -n   *job advisement service*

die Berufslaufbahn, -en   *career course*

die Berufsmöglichkeit, -en   *career possibility*

die Berufswahl   *career choice*

der Besuch, -e   *attendance, visit*

der Elektriker, -   *electrician*

die Entwicklung, -en   *development*

der Facharbeiter, -   *skilled worker, specialist*

die Fachschule, -n   *trade school*

die Firma, -men   *firm*

der Friseur, -e   *hair dresser*

die Grundlage, -n   *basis*

das Gymnasium, -ien   *school attended from ages 10–19*

der Handwerker, -   *artisan, craftsman*

die Hauptschule, -n   *school attended from ages 6–10 or 6–15*

die Hochschule, -n   *college, university*

der Ingenieur, -e   *engineer*

das Jahrhundert, -e   *century*

die Krankenschwester, -n   *nurse*

der Landwirt, -e   *farmer*

das Lehrjahr, -e   *year of apprenticeship*

der Maler, -   *painter*

der Maurer, -   *mason*

der Mechaniker, -   *mechanic*

73

die ,,Mittlere Reife" *diploma from German "Realschule"*
das Monatsgehalt, ̈er *monthly salary*
der Programmierer, - *programmer*
die Realschule, -n *school attended from ages 10–16*
der Richter, - *judge*
der Schneider, - *tailor*
die Schule, -n *school*
der Schüler, -, die Schülerin, -nen *pupil*
der Schuster, - *shoemaker*
die Sekretärin, -nen *secretary*
der Selbständige, -n *self-employed person*
das Staatsexamen, -ina *diploma from a university*
das Studium, -ien *study, attendance at a university*

die Technik, -en *technology*
der Techniker, - *technician*
der Tischler, - *cabinetmaker*
die Universität, -en *university*
die Verkäuferin, -nen *saleslady*
der Wissenschaftler, - *scientist*
der Wochenlohn, ̈e *weekly wages*

an·stellen *to hire*
beenden *to finish, conclude*
berechtigen *to entitle, justify*
ein·richten *to set up, arrange*

entscheiden, entschied, entschieden *to decide*
erhalten (erhält), erhielt, erhalten *to receive, obtain*
erleichtern *to make easy, alleviate*
ermöglichen *to make possible*
gründen *to establish, found*
schaffen, schuf, geschaffen *to create*
verdienen *to earn*
vor·ziehen, zog vor, vorgezogen *to prefer*

akademisch *academic*
beispielsweise *for example*
besonders *especially*
dreijährig *three–year*
eigen *own, individual*
einzeln *single, individual*
genau *exact*
mindestens *at least*
selber *himself, herself*
selbständig *independent(ly)*
täglich *daily*
wenig *little, few*
wichtig *important*
wissenschaftlich *scientific, scholarly*

ebenso wie *as well as*
einen Beruf aus·üben *to practice a profession*
einen Beruf erlangen *to acquire a profession*

ZUM BESPRECHEN

1. Warum gab es früher weniger Berufe als heute?
2. Welche Abschlüsse gibt es für deutsche Schulen?
3. Was muß ein Schüler nach dem Hauptschulabschluß machen, um Handwerker zu werden?
4. Vergleichen Sie die Berufslaufbahnen eines Polizisten und eines Arztes in Deutschland. Welche Schulen besucht man, um Polizist, welche um Arzt zu werden?
5. Erklären Sie den Unterschied zwischen einem Schüler und einem Studenten.
6. Wer erhält einen Monatsgehalt und wer erhält einen Wochenlohn in Deutschland?
7. Was ist ein Selbständiger?
8. Warum ist es oft schwer, den richtigen Beruf zu finden?
9. Wo kann man Auskunft über Berufe bekommen?

ZUR AUSFÜHRLICHEN DISKUSSION

1. Spielen Sie mit einem Kommilitonen die Rollen von deutschen und amerikanischen Studenten. Besprechen Sie die Unterschiede zwischen dem amerikanischen und dem deutschen Schulsystem.
2. Ziehen Sie das deutsche oder das amerikanische Schulsystem vor? Warum?
3. Berichten Sie über Ihren zukünftigen Beruf.

STUNDENPLAN

Fräulein _Ulrike Ute Ahrndsen_   Klasse: _5a_

Datum _den 10. Mai 1979_

Zimmer-Nr. _116_

Klassenleiter (in) _H. Schneider_

geboren am _05.07.1968_   zu _München_

römisch-katholischen   Bekenntnisses, wohnhaft in _München_

Stunde	Montag	Dienstag	Mittwoch	Donnerstag	Freitag
1 8-8:45	ERDKUNDE	HANDARBEIT	ENGLISCH FRANZÖSISCH	ENGLISCH	MATHEMATIK
2. 8:50-9:35	ENGLISCH FRANZÖSISCH	HANDARBEIT	RELIGION	MATHEMATIK	ENGLISCH FRANZÖSISCH
3. 9:40-10:15	MATHEMATIK	MATHEMATIK	BIOLOGIE	DEUTSCH	ENGLISCH FRANZÖSISCH
4. 10:45-11:30	MUSIK	DEUTSCH	ERDKUNDE	MUSIK	RELIGION
5. 11:35-12:20	SPORT: TURNEN	ENGLISCH FRANZÖSISCH	KUNST-ERZIEHUNG	DEUTSCH	SPORT: TURNEN
6. 12:25-13:10	DEUTSCH		KUNST-ERZIEHUNG	BIOLOGIE	

WORTSCHATZ

das Curriculum, -la   *curriculum*
die Erdkunde   *geography*
das Fach, ̈er   *subject*
die Handarbeit   *needlework*
die Kunsterziehung   *art education*

anspruchsvoll   *demanding, exacting*

ZUM BESPRECHEN

1. Wie alt ist Ulrike? In welcher Klasse ist sie?
2. Welche Fächer hat sie?
3. Ist der Schultag (in München) länger oder kürzer als bei Ihnen in der Schule?
4. Welche Unterschiede gibt es zwischen den Fächern, die Ulrike hat und den Fächern, die Sie in der fünften oder sechsten Klasse hatten?
5. Finden Sie Ulrikes Curriculum anspruchsvoller als an einer amerikanischen Schule? Warum?

ZEUGNIS

Schule *Willi-Graf-Gymnasium*   Schuljahr   *5a*

Fräulein   *Ulrike Uta Ahrndsen*

geboren am   *05.07. 1968*   zu   *München*

_____ *röm.-kath.* _____ Bekenntnisses.

wohnhaft in   *München*

Notenstufen: sehr gut   *(1)*   mangelhaft   *(5)*
               gut   *(2)*   ungenügend   *(6)*
               befriedigend   *(3)*
               ausreichend   *(4)*

Die Leistungen in den einzelnen Fächern sind wie folgt beurteilt worden:

Religionslehre . . . . *befriedigend*
Deutsch . . . . *befriedigend*
Latein . . . .
Englisch . . . . *mangelhaft*
Französisch . . . . *befriedigend*
Mathematik . . . . *sehr gut*
Naturwissenschaften
  Physik . . . .
  Chemie . . . .
  Biologie . . . . *sehr gut*
Gemeinschaftskunde
  Geschichte . . . . *ausreichend*
  Erdkunde . . . . *gut*
  Sozialkunde . . . .
Ethik . . . .
Kunsterziehung . . . . *ungenügend*
Musik . . . . *ungenügend*
Sport . . . . *sehr gut*

GRADING LEVELS

(1) sehr gut *very good*
(2) gut *good*
(3) befriedigend *satisfactory*
(4) ausreichend *adequate*
(5) mangelhaft *deficient*
(6) ungenügend *unsatisfactory*

WORTSCHATZ

das Bekenntnis, -se *confession*
die Gemeinschaftskunde *social studies*
die Leistung, -en *performance*
die Naturwissenschaft, -en *natural science*
die Note, -n *grade*
das Zeugnis, -se *report card*

beurteilen *to evaluate*

schließen, schloß, geschlossen *to conclude, dose*

mittelmäßig *mediocre*
schwach *weak*
wohnhaft in *domicile in*

das stimmt *that's right*

ZUM BESPRECHEN

1. Unterscheidet sich das Notensystem in Deutschland von dem in Amerika?
2. Welche Note ist die beste in Deutschland? Welche ist die schlechteste? Welche Noten sind mittelmäßig?
3. Was sind Ulrikes beste Fächer? Was sind ihre schwächsten Fächer? In welchen Fächern ist Ihre Leistung mittelmäßig?
4. Glauben Sie, daß Ulrike eine gute Schülerin ist?
5. Welche Abschlußprüfung muß Ulrike mit 19 Jahren machen?
6. Welches Hauptfach und welches Nebenfach wird Ulrike wahrscheinlich an der Universität studieren? Woraus schließen Sie das?

ZUR AUSFÜHRLICHEN DISKUSSION

1. Sind Sie ein guter Student oder eine gute Studentin? Warum oder warum nicht?
2. Haben Sie als Schüler(in) gute oder schlechte Noten bekommen? Welches war Ihr schwächstes Fach? Ihr bestes Fach? Sprechen Sie mit Ihren Kommilitonen über Ihre früheren Schuljahre.
3. Stimmt das amerikanische Sprichwort „Noten sind nicht alles"? Begründen Sie Ihre Antwort!

Beschreiben Sie diese Klasse in dem Willi–Graf–Mädchen–Gymnasium in München.

AUF DEM BAHNHOF

9

WORTSCHATZ

der Bahnhof, ⸚e *railway station*
das Buffet, -s *buffet, snack bar*
das Getränk, -e *drink*
die Lokomotive, -n *engine*
die Reise, -n *trip*
der Reiseproviant *travel provisions*
die Schwierigkeit, -en *difficulty*
die Speise, -n *food*
das Telefon, -e *telephone*
die Telefonzelle, -n *telephone booth*
die Uhr, -en *clock*
der Wagen, - *car (of trains also)*
der Zug, ⸚e *train*

ab·fahren (fährt ab), fuhr ab, ist
 abgefahren *to leave, depart*
ab·holen *to pick up*
an·kommen, kam an, ist
 angekommen *to arrive*
telefonieren mit *to call up, telephone*

bald *soon*
nötig *necessary*

gerade angekommen *just arrived*

ZUM BESPRECHEN

1. Beschreiben Sie die Szene auf Seite 78.
2. Wieviel Uhr ist es? Warum ist es wichtig, daß im Bahnhof eine Uhr hängt?
3. Wie viele Züge sehen Sie auf dem Bild? Welche Züge sind gerade angekommen? Woher wissen Sie das? Welche Züge fahren wahrscheinlich bald ab?
4. Wo kann man telefonieren? Warum ist es nötig, am Bahnhof Telefone zu haben?
5. Warum ist es praktisch, wenn es im Bahnhof ein kaltes Buffet gibt? Welche Speisen und Getränke kann man dort kaufen?
6. Sie sind gerade im Hauptbahnhof München angekommen. Telefonieren Sie mit Ihrem Freund, der Sie vom Bahnhof abholen sollte. Ein Klassenkamerad spielt die Rolle Ihres Freundes. Besprechen Sie, was Sie machen werden, wenn es Schwierigkeiten gibt.

Auf dem Bahnsteig

WORTSCHATZ

die Gaststätte, -n *restaurant*
das Gepäck *luggage*
der Koffer, - *suitcase*
der Koffer-Kuli, -s *luggage cart*
die Mütze, -n *cap*
die Post, (-ämter) *post office*
das Schließfach, ¨er *locker*
die Stunde, -n *hour*
der Wartesaal, -säle *waiting room*

schieben, schob, geschoben *to push*
warten auf (+ *acc.*) *to wait for*

manchmal *frequently*
nützlich *useful*
unentbehrlich *indispensable*

ZUM BESPRECHEN

1. Was macht der Mann mit der Mütze?
2. Warum ist ein Koffer-Kuli manchmal unentbehrlich?
3. Wann benutzt man ein Schließfach?
4. Warum ist es nützlich, wenn es im Bahnhof eine Post gibt?
5. Warum muß es im Bahnhof einen Wartesaal geben?
6. Was packen Sie ein, wenn Sie übers Wochenende in die Berge fahren?
7. Was kann man am Bahnhof machen, wenn man drei Stunden auf den Zug warten muß?

WORTSCHATZ

die Abfahrtszeit, -en *time of departure*
die Ankunftszeit, -en *time of arrival*
der Bahnsteig, -e *railway platform*
die (Eisen)bahn, -en *railroad*
die Eisenbahnfahrt, -en *train trip*
das Gleis, -e *track*
der Güterzug, ⁼e *freight train*
der Schnellzug, ⁼e *express train*

der Zielbahnhof, ⁼e *station of destination*

auf dem Schild stehen *to be on the sign*
mit der Bahn fahren *to travel by train*
woher? *where from?*
wohin? *where to?*

ZUM BESPRECHEN

1. Auf welchem Gleis steht der Zug?
2. Woher kommt der Zug?
3. In welcher Stadt und in welchem Land liegt der Zielbahnhof des Zuges?
4. Durch welche Städte fährt der Zug, bevor er in München ankommt?
5. Wann kommt der Zug an? Wann fährt der Zug ab? Woher wissen Sie das?
6. Was ist der Unterschied zwischen einem Schnellzug und einem Güterzug?
7. Beschreiben Sie Ihre letzte Eisenbahnfahrt.
8. Ist die Eisenbahn in Europa populärer als in Amerika?

81

D 4 München—Salzburg—**Graz** und Villach—**Klagenfurt/Triest** und **Venedig**

			D 211	D 1683 E 3527		D 1393	D 265	D 293	D 1395	D 1415	E 3517	D 295	D 411	D 297	D 667	D 9337	D 9393	D 9313	D 9317	D 9319
Hamburg Hbf		ab	15 05	17 40	8 10		8 10		11 40				13 45		14 00		01204	01530			
Hannover Hbf	8		18 02	19 19	10.06		10 06		13 10				15 16		15 40		01516	01750			
Nürnberg Hbf 80			12 57			13 56				16 50		18 12		19 15			21 46				
München Hbf		an	14 55	15 09	16 18	15 53		16 18		19 12	19 29	20 13		21 15	21 11	22 07			②		
Köln Hbf 2.3		ab		8 03		9 19	10 55		13 00				13 05	15 28			17 00			01809	018 09
Frankfurt (M) Hbf 80.90		ab					13 14	12 30			16 56	17 24	17 05	14 54	19 58	19 37	20 25	2059		20 53	2053	2053
Stuttgart Hbf 90				12 47				14 53	14 39		19 08	19 58	19 44	20 30	21 21	2227	22 12	2255	2313	2339	2339	2339
München Hbf		an		15 15			16 57	17 01	17 09	17 04												

km		950	Zug Nr															S	T	U	V	W
0	**München** Hbf	ab	15 34	16 33			17 19	17 25	17 30	19 52	20 15	20 26	20 50	21 38	22 45	23 26						
65	Rosenheim	950 ab	16 18	17 17			18 58	1904	19 11	20 50		21 56	22 29	22 37	23 22	0 28	1 14						
153	Salzburg Hbf	an	17 32	18 38																			

		Zug Nr		D 542			E 644						D 466		D 546	D 567					
153	Salzburg Hbf	ab	18.08	18 50	19 20		19 30	19 50	22 12	22 26		23 05	23 50	23 45	0 52	2 08						
172	Hallein	23020 an		18 32	19 08			20 10															
183	Golling-Abtenau	23040 an	18 32	19 08											0 35	0 30							
207	Bischofshofen	an	18 54		19 38		20 04		20 14	20 40	22 57					2 53							

207	Bischofshofen	ab															4 30				
224	Eben i. Pongau	an															4 53				
231	Radstadt	an															5 10				
250	Schladming	an															5 23				
269	Gröbming	an															5 43				
290	Stainach-Irdning	an															5 54				
303	Liezen	an															6 01				
309	Selzthal	an						MOZART			TAUERN-ORIENT	⑥ vom 24., 25., 26. VI. bis 16., 17., IX.	JUGOSLAVIA-EXPRESS	HELLAS-EXPRESS	WIENER WALZER	MOSTAR-DALMACIA						
315	Stadt Rottenmann	23030 an																			
326	Trieben	an																			
342	Wald a Schoberpass	an																			
349	Kalwang	an																			
357	Mautern	an																			
372	St Michael	an															7 04				
382	Leoben Hbf	an															7 20				
398	Bruck a d Mur	an																			
452	**Graz** Hbf	an															8 10				

207	Bischofshofen	23020 an	18 59		19 40		20 05	20 18	20 48	22 58			0 37	0 46	3 03						
216	St Johann i Pongau	23040 an	19 07						20 56							78143					
221	Schwarzach-StVeit	an	19 14		19 56		20 20	20 34	21 03	23 13	23 25		0 05	0 51	1 00	1 52	3 18	2				
	Schwarzach-StVeit	ab	19 33		19 58				21 10						1 03	3 27						
	Zell am See	23040 an	20 13		20 28				21 45						1 33	3 58						
	Saalfelden	an	20 30		20 39				21 59							4 15						

221	Schwarzach-St Veit	an	19 25		20 23		20 40		23 17	23 30		0 10	0 56		2 04	4 40					
236	Dorfgastein	an	19 41						22 37							4 57					
241	Hofgastein	an	19 51						23 50	0 01						5 12					
252	Badgastein	an	20 04					21 11								5 29					
256	Böckstein	an	20 14													6 14					
268	Mallnitz	23020 an	20 29					21 32								6 28					
274	Obervellach	an						835								6 36					
287	Kolbnitz	an	20 50													6 55					
292	Mühldorf-Möllbrücke	an	20 57					ab								7 02					
304	Spittal-Millstättersee	an	21 10		21 44	21 52	22 10							3 31		7 15					
	Spittal-Millstätters	23021 ab	21 47											5 32	9 31						
	Lienz	an	23 07											6 45	10 50						
341	Villach Hbf	23020 an	21 45		22 16	22 20	22 49	1 13	1 31	2 10	3 00		4 00		8 16	6 40	6 40	8 05	8 05	8 05	
	Villach Hbf														5 21	8 35					
	Feldkirchen i. K.	23022 an													5 55	9 08					

		Zug Nr					232									7 534	4222				
341	Villach Hbf	ab	21 56				2 19						4 50	8 40					
357	Velden am Wörthersee	an	22 10										5 00	8 58					
365	Pörtschach a W	23020 an	22 17										5 06	9 07					
371	Krumpendorf	an	22 23										5 12	9 15					
379	**Klagenfurt** Hbf	an	22 30				2 43						5 20	9 24					

		Zug Nr					233						4803 2					
341	Villach Hbf	ab											4 40	6 50				
359	Arnoldstein MEZ	23070 an											4 57	9 15				
369	Tarvisio Centr OEZ	an											6 14	1030				

		Zug Nr						(233)(2623)						
369	Tarvisio Centr OEZ	ab						6 37						
463	Udine	an						8 18						

463	Udine	ab							8 45					
546	**Trieste** Centr	24506 an							9 56					

463	Udine	ab						8 26					
590	Venezia Mestre	an						10 10					
579	**Venezia** S Lucia	an						10 26					

= der Kurswagen,— 　　= der Liegewagen,— 　　= Speisen und Getränke

= der Schlafwagen,— 　　= der Speisewagen,— 　　= der Grenzbahnhof, ˙˙e

Der Fahrplan

WORTSCHATZ

die Entfernung, -en *distance*
der Fahrplan, ⸚e *timetable*
die Grenze, -n *border*
der Kurswagen, - *passenger car destined for a certain city*
der Liegewagen, - *couchette (less luxurious than a **Schlafwagen**)*
der Schlafwagen, - *sleeping car*
der Speisewagen, - *dining car*
das Wandern *hiking*

unterbrechen (unterbricht), unterbrach, unterbrochen *to interrupt*

an der Grenze *at the border*
den Paß vor·zeigen *to show one's passport*
durch den Zoll gehen *to go through customs*

ZUM BESPRECHEN

1. Wann kommt der D211 aus München in Klagenfurt an?
2. Kann man im D211 essen, wenn man hungrig wird? Woher wissen Sie das?
3. Wann kann man von München nach Klagenfurt fahren, wenn man im Zug schlafen will? Wann kommt man in Klagenfurt an? Hat der Zug einen Namen?
4. Welcher Bahnhof ist der Grenzbahnhof zwischen München und Klagenfurt? Was muß man an der Grenze machen?
5. Wie groß ist die Entfernung zwischen München und Klagenfurt?
6. Sie planen mit Ihrem Freund eine Reise von München nach Villach zum Wandern. Sie möchten aber auch einige Stunden mit Ihren Verwandten in Salzburg verbringen. Planen Sie mit Ihrem Partner eine Reise, die Sie für einige Stunden in Salzburg unterbrechen können.

"Am Fahrkartenschalter"

WORTSCHATZ

das Ausland *foreign country, abroad*
die Fahrkarte, -n *ticket;* die einfache
  Fahrkarte, -n *one-way ticket*
der Fahrkartenschalter, - *ticket
    window*
das Inland *inland, domestic*
die Rückfahrkarte, -n *round-trip ticket*
der Schalter, - *ticket window, counter*
der Schalterbeamte, -n, -n *ticket agent*
der Tourist, -en, -en *tourist*

benutzen *to use*
reisen, ist gereist *to travel*
sich überlegen (dat.) *to consider,
    reflect*

geöffnet *open*
geschlossen *closed*

erster Klasse fahren *to travel first class*
zweiter Klasse fahren *to travel coach*

ZUM BESPRECHEN

1. Welche Schalter sind geöffnet und welche sind geschlossen? Woher wissen Sie das?
2. Wo sitzt der Schalterbeamte?
3. Was macht der Beamte hinter dem geschlossenen Schalter?
4. Stellen Sie sich vor, was die Frau, die am Schalter steht, sagen könnte.
5. Was überlegt sich der Mann, der links steht? Benutzen Sie Ihre Phantasie!
6. Spielen Sie mit einem Klassenkameraden die Rollen von Touristen und Fahrkarten-
   beamten. Kaufen Sie eine Fahrkarte (erster Klasse? zweiter Klasse?) nach einer Stadt
   im Ausland. Stellen Sie so viele Fragen wie möglich!

Im Verkehrsbüro

WORTSCHATZ

die Information, -en; die Auskunft,
ᵉe *information*
das Stadtverkehrsbüro, -s *city
information office*
das Verkehrsbüro, -s *information
bureau*

der Zimmernachweis, -e *room
information*

Informationen geben *to provide
information*

ZUM BESPRECHEN

1. Warum ist es für Touristen gut, wenn es im Bahnhof a) einen Zimmernachweis und
   b) ein Stadtverkehrsbüro gibt?
2. Spielen Sie die Rollen von Touristen und Angestellten des Verkehrsbüros. Stellen Sie
   so viele Fragen wie möglich über die Stadt und die Hotels, in denen Sie übernachten
   können.

Der Gepäckwagen

WORTSCHATZ

das Fahrrad, ⸚er *bicycle*
der Gepäckwagen, - *baggage car*
der Schaffner, - *conductor*

entladen (entlädt), entlud, entladen *to unload*
rad·fahren (fährt Rad), fuhr Rad, ist radgefahren *to ride a bicycle*

ZUM BESPRECHEN

1. Was macht der Schaffner auf dem Bild?
2. Welche anderen Pflichten hat ein Schaffner?
3. Warum ist es vorteilhaft, ein Fahrrad auf einer Reise im Gepäckwagen mitzunehmen?

Der Kurswagen

WORTSCHATZ

der Kurswagen, - *passenger car (of train) destined for a certain city*
der Nichtraucher *non-smoker*
der Rauch *smoke*
der Raucher *smoker*

aus·steigen, stieg aus, ist ausgestiegen *to get off, disembark*
ein·steigen, stieg ein, ist eingestiegen *to get on, board*

ZUM BESPRECHEN

1. Steigen diese Reisenden ein oder steigen sie aus?
2. Machen die Leute auf dem Bild eine lange oder eine kurze Reise?
3. Was bedeutet die Aufschrift „Nichtraucher"?
4. Wohin fährt dieser Kurswagen? Wo kommt er her? Woher wissen Sie das?
5. Fahren diese Reisenden erster Klasse oder zweiter Klasse? Woher wissen Sie das?

Der Buffetwagen

ZUM BESPRECHEN

1. Beschreiben Sie das Bild!
2. Was kann man vom Buffetwagen kaufen?
3. Warum ist ein Buffetwagen praktisch?

Im Speisewagen

ZUM BESPRECHEN

1. Beschreiben Sie die Szene auf dem Bild!
2. Warum ist es angenehm, im Speisewagen zu essen? Gibt es auch Gründe, die gegen ein Essen im Speisewagen sprechen?

IM KAUFHAUS 10

Ein Kaufhaus wird auch Warenhaus genannt. In Deutschland bietet ein Kaufhaus nicht nur über hunderttausend verschiedene Artikel oder Waren an, sondern man kann dort auch Lebensmittel kaufen.

Damit sich nun jeder Käufer in einem Warenhaus gut zurechtfinden kann, gibt es die Verkaufsabteilungen. Sie sind in mehreren Stockwerken untergebracht. Auf Rolltreppen oder mit Fahrstühlen kann man zu den einzelnen Abteilungen gelangen. In der Spielwarenabteilung werden nur Spielwaren verkauft, in der Lebensmittelabteilung nur Lebensmittel. Außerdem gibt es Verkaufsabteilungen für Sportsachen, für Damen- und Herrenbekleidung, für Bücher, für Schuhe, für Werkzeuge, für Haushaltsgeräte, für Möbel, für Schmuck und für viele andere Dinge.

Außer den Verkaufsabteilungen gibt es aber auch noch andere Einrichtungen in einem Kaufhaus: Cafés, Imbißstuben oder Restaurants. Die meisten Kaufhäuser haben auch einen Kindergarten. Dort werden die Kinder beaufsichtigt, während die Mütter ungestört einkaufen können.

In den Kaufhäusern kann man billige und teure Waren kaufen. Oft haben die Leute aber nicht genug Geld, um beispielsweise einen Farbfernseher oder eine Waschmaschine auf einmal zu bezahlen. Deshalb gibt es in den meisten Warenhäusern die

Möglichkeit, teure Gegenstände auf Raten zu kaufen. Das heißt, man zahlt einen Teil des Kaufpreises an; der Rest wird dann in Teilbeträgen, das sind die Raten, bezahlt. Wenn ein Farbfernseher für 2000 Mark gekauft wird, dann kann man 200 Mark anzahlen und das Gerät mitnehmen. Die restlichen 1800 Mark werden in 9 Raten zu je 200 Mark aufgeteilt. Man unterschreibt einen Ratenzahlungsvertrag. Darin steht, in welchem Zeitraum das restliche Geld bezahlt werden muß. Einen solchen Vertrag dürfen nur Personen unterschreiben, die mindestens 18 Jahre alt sind.

Die Einrichtung und Instandhaltung eines Kaufhausgebäudes kostet sehr viel Geld. Deshalb gibt es Kaufhäuser gewöhnlich nur in Großstädten. Der Betrieb eines Kaufhauses lohnt sich nur, wenn viele Leute dort einkaufen.

WORTSCHATZ

der Artikel, - *article*
der Betrieb *operation*
die Damenbekleidung *women's clothing*
das Ding, -e *thing*
die Einrichtung, -en *furnishing*
der Fahrstuhl, ⸚e *elevator*
der Farbfernseher, - *color TV*
das Haushaltsgerät, -e *household appliance*
die Herrenbekleidung *men's clothing*
die Imbißstube, -n *snack bar*
die Instandhaltung *maintenance*
der Käufer, - *buyer*
das Kaufhaus, ⸚er *department store*
der Kindergarten, ⸚ *kindergarten*
die Lebensmittel (*pl.*) *groceries*
die Möbel (*pl.*) *furniture*
die Rate, -n *installment*
der Ratenzahlungsvertrag, ⸚e *installment payment contract*
der Rest, -e *rest, remainder*
das Restaurant, -s *restaurant*
die Rolltreppe, -n *escalator*
der Schmuck *jewelry*
der Schuh, -e *shoe*
die Spielwaren (*pl.*) *toys*
die Sportsachen (*pl.*) *sporting goods*
das Stockwerk, -e *story, floor*
der Teilbetrag, ⸚e *installment*
die Verkaufsabteilung, -en *sales department*
die Ware, -n *article*
das Warenhaus, ⸚er *department store*
die Waschmaschine, -n *washing machine*

das Werkzeug, -e *tool*
der Zeitraum, ⸚e *period of time*

an·zahlen *to make a down payment*
auf·teilen *to divide up*
beaufsichtigen *to watch, supervise*
besitzen *to own*
bezahlen *to pay*
ein·kaufen *to shop*
gelangen zu *to reach, arrive at*
kaufen *to buy*
sich lohnen *to be worthwhile*
mit·nehmen (nimmt mit), nahm mit, mitgenommen *to take along*
nennen, nannte, genannt *to name*
unterschreiben, unterschrieb, unterschrieben *to sign*
sich zurecht·finden, fand sich zurecht, sich zurechtgefunden *to find one's way about*

beispielsweise *for example*
billig *inexpensive*
mindestens *at least*
restlich *remaining*
richtig *right*
ungestört *undisturbed*
untergebracht *to be arranged, housed*

anhand (+ *gen.*) *with the aid of*
auf einmal *at once, immediately*
auf Raten kaufen *to buy on the installment plan*
damit *so that (conj.)*
es gibt (+ *acc.*) *there is, there are*
zu je 200 Mark *at 200 marks each*

91

ZUM BESPRECHEN

1. Was findet man in einem deutschen Kaufhaus?
2. Wozu braucht man eine Rolltreppe oder einen Fahrstuhl in einem Kaufhaus?
3. Warum gibt es so viele Verkaufsabteilungen in einem Kaufhaus? Nennen Sie einige.
4. Welche Einrichtungen gibt es außer den Verkaufsabteilungen?
5. Warum haben manche Kaufhäuser einen Kindergarten?
6. Was kann man tun, wenn man etwas nicht auf einmal bezahlen kann? Erklären Sie das anhand eines Beispiels!
7. Kann jeder einen Ratenzahlungsvertrag unterschreiben? Warum?
8. Warum gibt es Kaufhäuser meistens nur in Großstädten?

ZUR AUSFÜHRLICHEN DISKUSSION

1. Wie unterscheidet sich ein deutsches Kaufhaus von einem amerikanischen Kaufhaus? Inwiefern sind sie gleich?
2. Nennen Sie einige Vor- und Nachteile von Ratenkäufen.
3. Beschreiben Sie Ihrem Partner in der Klasse den teuersten Gegenstand, den Sie je gekauft haben.

Die Verkaufsabteilungen

ERDGESCHOSS

4. OBERGESCHOSS
Möbel -
Restaurant · Fernsprecher
Alles für's Bad

3. OBERGESCHOSS
Rundfunk · Fernsehen · Lampen
Klein- u. Großelektro · Herde · Öfen
Haushaltwaren · Geschenkartikel
Werkzeuge · Do it yourself
Autozubehör · Zweiräder ·
· Glas · Porzellan
FKB-Bank
NECKURA-Versicherungen

2. OBERGESCHOSS
Alles fürs Kind · Sport · Camping
Spielwaren · Kundendienst
Gardinen · Dekostoffe · Teppiche
Baumwollwaren Bettwaren

1. OBERGESCHOSS
Damenoberbekleidung
Herrenoberbekleidung
Damenwäsche · Miederwaren
Strickwaren · Nähmaschinen
Schuhe · Lederwaren
Schürzen · · Handarbeiten
Modewaren · Kleinpelze

ERDGESCHOSS
Parfümerie · Schmuck · Uhren
Schreib- Rechenmaschinen · Bücher
Schreibwaren · Herrenhüte · Schirme
Damen- u. Herrenstrümpfe
Wäsche · Herrenartikel · Tabakwaren
NUR-Reisebüro
Schnellfoto
Foto · Optik · Schallplatten

KELLERGESCHOSS
Lebensmittel
Putz- u. Waschmittel
Toto · Lotto · Zeitschriften

das Geschoß das Stockwerk *floor, story*
der Fernsprecher *telephone*

der Rundfunk   *radio*
Elektro   *electrical;* der Herd *range;* der Ofen *oven*
die Haushaltswaren *(pl.)   household articles;* das Geschenk *present*
das Werkzeug   *tool*
das Autozubehör   *auto accessories;* die Zweiräder *(pl.) two-wheelers*
das Porzellan   *china*
die Bank   *bank*
die Versicherung   *insurance*

der Kundendienst   *customer service*
die Gardine   *curtain;* der Stoff   *fabric;* der Teppich *rug*
die Baumwollwaren *(pl.)   cottons; Bettwaren (pl.) bed articles*

die Oberbekleidung   *outer-wear*
die Damenwäsche   *lingerie;* Miederwaren *(pl.) foundation garments*
die Strickwaren *(pl.)   knitware;* die Nähmaschine *sewing machine*
die Lederwaren *(pl.)   leather goods*
die Schürze   *apron;* die Handarbeit *needlework*
die Modewaren *(pl.)   fashions;* der Pelz *fur*

die Parfümerie   *cosmetics department;* die Uhr *clock, watch*
die Schreibmaschine   *typewriter;* die Rechenmaschine *calculator*
die Schreibwaren *(pl.)   stationery;* der Hut *hat;* der Schirm *umbrella*
der Strumpf   *sock, stocking*
die Wäsche   *linens;* Tabakwaren *(pl.) tobacco articles*
das Reisebüro   *travel agency;* Schnellfoto *quick foto service;* Optik *optics;* die Schallplatte *record, record album*

der Keller   *basement*
die Putz- und Waschmittel *(pl.)   scouring and dishwashing detergents*
das Toto-Lotto   *lottery;* die Zeitschrift *magazine*

93

ZUM BESPRECHEN

1. In welchem Stockwerk ist das Foto (Seite 93) aufgenommen?
2. In welcher Verkaufsabteilung und in welchem Stockwerk finden Sie die folgenden Artikel?

   a.) einen Hammer
   b.) einen Farbfernseher
   c.) Batterien
   d.) ein Handtuch
   e.) eine Waschmaschine
   f.) ein Geschenk für Ihren Neffen
   g.) eine Filmkamera
   h.) eine Stereoanlage
   i.) ein Hemd für Ihren Vater
   j.) Papier
   k.) eine Illustrierte

   l.) einen Fußball
   m.) eine Ledertasche
   n.) Nagellack
   o.) etwas für Ihre Mutter
   p.) Wein
   q.) ein Kissen
   r.) einen Schlafsack
   s.) ein Motorrad
   t.) Informationen über Flüge nach Amerika
   u.) einen Farbfilm

3. Warum ist es gut, wenn es eine Bank im Warenhaus gibt?
4. Was für Versicherungen gibt es in der Versicherungsabteilung? Gibt es diese Abteilung auch in amerikanischen Warenhäusern? Warum ist das eine gute Idee?
5. Wohin geht man, wenn man Informationen über Ratenzahlung erhalten will?
6. In welchem Stockwerk würden Sie die meiste Zeit verbringen? In welchem würden Sie die wenigste Zeit verbringen? Warum?
7. Sie und Ihr Partner in der Klasse haben DM 200 000 im Toto-Lotto gewonnen. Besprechen Sie, was Sie im Warenhaus kaufen wollen.

Beim Schlußverkauf

WORTSCHATZ

die Größe, -n   *size*
die Kasse, -n   *cashier's desk, cash register*
das Oberhemd, -en   *dress shirt*
der Schlußverkauf, ⁼e   *final bargain sale (in winter and summer in Germany)*
das T-Shirt, -s   *T-shirt*
die Verkäuferin, -nen   *saleslady*

an·probieren   *to try on*
aus·suchen   *to choose*
passen (+ *dat.*)   *to fit*
um·tauschen   *to exchange*

vermutlich   *probably*

sicher sein   *to be certain*

ZUM BESPRECHEN

1. Wie heißt das Warenhaus auf dem Bild (Seite 94)?
2. Wo steht die Verkäuferin? Was macht sie vermutlich?
3. Was tut der Mann rechts?
4. Was tun die Damen links?
5. Wie kann man sicher sein, daß ein Kleidungsstück paßt?
6. In welcher Verkaufsabteilung befinden sich die Leute auf dem Foto?
7. Sie bekommen drei Hemden als Geschenk von Ihrer Mutter. Leider haben sie alle die falsche Größe. Was können Sie tun? Was tun Sie, wenn Sie erfahren, daß die Hemden im Schlußverkauf gekauft wurden?

Die Kreditkarte

WORTSCHATZ

das Bargeld   *cash*
das Büro, -s   *office*
die Kreditkarte, -n   *credit card*
die Unterschrift, -en   *signature*

gelten (gilt), galt, gegolten   *to be valid*
lassen (läßt), ließ, gelassen   *to leave, let*
sich informieren   *to inform oneself*

ZUM BESPRECHEN

1. Für welches Warenhaus gilt die Kreditkarte auf Seite 95?
2. Warum heißt die Karte die „Anstatt–Geld Karte"?
3. Was findet man im 2. Stock?
4. Erklären Sie: „Zahlen Sie mit Ihrer Unterschrift."
5. Nennen Sie einige Vor– und Nachteile einer Kreditkarte.

In der Fernsehabteilung

WORTSCHATZ

der Batteriebetrieb	*battery operation*	massenweise	*en masse, in large numbers*
das Fernsehgerät, -e	*TV set*	toll	*crazy, neat (idiom.)*
das Schlagwort, -e	*slogan*	tragbar	*portable*
kosten	*to cost*		

ZUM BESPRECHEN

1. Warum kostet das eine Fernsehgerät DM 229,- und das andere DM 848, -?
2. Erklären Sie das Schlagwort „tolle Preise massenweise".
3. Warum ist es gut, ein tragbares Fernsehgerät zu kaufen?
4. Warum ist es praktisch, ein Fernsehgerät mit 12V-Batteriebetrieb zu haben?

1. Für die Dame

2.

WORTSCHATZ

das Armband, ⸚er *bracelet*
der Blitz, -e *lightning flash*
der Mantel, ⸚ *coat*
die Möglichkeit, -en *possibility*
der Ohrring, -e *earring*
die Restbestände (*pl.*) *remnants*
der Schmuck *jewelry*
die Strumpfhose, -n *panty hose*

ein·schlagen (schlägt ein), schlug ein,
  eingeschlagen *to strike (like
  lightning)*
vor·schlagen (schlägt vor), schlug vor,
  vorgeschlagen *to suggest*

Vorschläge machen *to make
  suggestions*

ZUM BESPRECHEN

1. Welche Verkaufsabteilungen sind auf den Bildern (Seite 97) dargestellt? Welche Sachen kann man hier kaufen?
2. Was tun die Damen auf den Bildern?
3. Warum sollte eine Dame im Sommer einen Pelzmantel kaufen?
4. Erkären Sie das Schlagwort „Blitz: Angebote, die einschlagen"! (*Bild 1*)
5. Würden Sie Restbestände kaufen (*Bild 2*)? Warum oder warum nicht?
6. Spielen Sie mit Ihrem Partner in der Klasse die Rollen von Kunden und Verkäuferin in der Damenabteilung eines großen Warenhauses. Sie möchten ein Geschenk für Ihre Mutter oder Ihre Freundin kaufen, aber Sie wissen nicht was. Die Verkäuferin macht Ihnen verschiedene Vorschläge.

„Einfach ein Erlebnis"

WORTSCHATZ

der Ausverkauf   *sale (prices reduced)*
der Bettbezug, ⸚e   *bed linen*
das Bettuch, ⸚er   *sheet*
die Bettwäsche   *bed linen*
das Erlebnis, -se   *experience,*
   adventure

der Kunde, -n, -n   *customer*
das Werbeplakat, -e   *advertisement*
   poster

einfach   *simple, simply*
reduziert   *reduced*

ZUM BESPRECHEN

1. Welche Verkaufsabteilung ist auf diesem Bild (Seite 98) dargestellt? Begründen Sie
   Ihre Antwort!
2. Warum sieht man so viele Kunden in dieser Abteilung?
3. „Karstadt— einfach ein Erlebnis!" Erklären Sie dieses Schlagwort. Warum sind ein
   kleines Mädchen und eine ältere Dame auf den Werbeplakaten zu sehen?

In der Lebensmittelabteilung

In der Fleischabteilung

WORTSCHATZ

der Einkaufswagen, - *shopping cart*
das Gramm *gram (100 g = 3.5 ounces)*
das Inserat, -e *advertisement*
der Kittel, - *smock*
der Ladentisch, -e *counter*
die Lebensmittel (*pl.*) *groceries*
der Markt, ̈e *market*

der Metzger, - *butcher*
das Schweinefleisch *pork*
das Steak, -s *steak*

schneiden, schnitt, geschnitten *to cut*

scharf rechnen *to calculate carefully*

100 ZUM BESPRECHEN

1. Wo steht der Metzger? Woran erkennen Sie, daß er Metzger ist?
2. Was tut der Metzger wahrscheinlich?
3. Beschreiben Sie die Kundinnen.

4. Woher wissen Sie, daß die Schweinesteaks billiger als gewöhnlich sind?
5. Wann gebraucht man einen Einkaufswagen?
6. Warum muß man im Lebensmittelgeschäft „scharf rechnen"?
7. Geben Sie einige Tips, wie man preiswert Lebensmittel einkaufen kann.

Ladendiebstahl

WORTSCHATZ

der Besitzer, - *owner*
die Höhe *amount*
der Ladendieb, -e *shoplifter*
der Ladendiebstahl *shoplifting*
die Maßnahme, -n *measure, precaution*
der Schadenersatz *damages*
das Schild, -er *sign*
der Schluß, ̈sse *end, finish*
die Straftat, -en *punishable offense*

entstehen, entstand, ist entstanden *to arise*

sich lohnen *to be worthwhile*
mit·zahlen *to share the cost*
schwarz·fahren, fuhr schwarz, ist schwarzgefahren *to ride (bus, subway) illegally without paying*

eine Strafanzeige erstatten gegen jemanden *to make a report to police against someone regarding a punishable offense*

101

ZUM BESPRECHEN

1. Erklären Sie: „Ladendiebstahl lohnt sich nicht." (Seite 101) Und „Ladendiebstahl und Schwarzfahren. Jetzt Schluß damit, denn Sie zahlen immer mit."
2. Bedeutet das rechte Schild, daß der Ladendieb nur DM 50, - für seine Straftat bezahlen muß?
3. Besprechen Sie das Problem des Ladendiebstahls. Beschreiben Sie die Folgen a) für den Ladendieb b) den Besitzer c) den Kunden.

An der Kasse

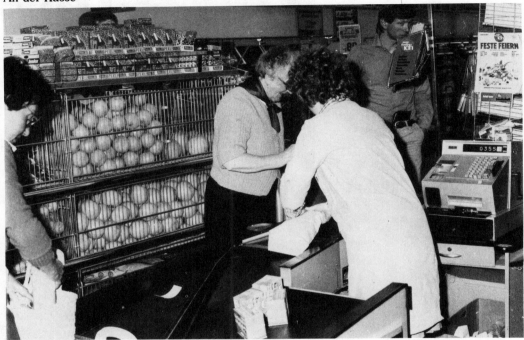

WORTSCHATZ

der Betrieb *activity, bustle; operation*
das Fest, -e *festival, banquet*
die Frucht, ⸚e; das Obst *fruit*
die Kasse, -n *check-out counter, cashier's desk*
die Kassiererin, -nen *cashier, checker*
der Korb, ⸚e *basket*
das Lebensmittelgeschäft, -e *grocery store*
die Lösung, -en *solution*
das Paket, -e *package*
die Registrierkasse, -n *cash register*
das Rezept, -e *recipe, prescription*
der Supermarkt, ⸚e *supermarket*

die Tasche, -n *purse, handbag; pocket*
die Tüte, -n; der Sack, ⸚e *bag*

sich an·stellen *to stand in line*
bemerken *to notice*
ein·packen *to pack*
feiern *to celebrate*
herrschen *to reign, prevail, rule*

die Beträge zusammen·zählen *to add up the bill*
Geld bei sich haben *to have money with you*

102

ZUM BESPRECHEN

1. Was macht die Kassiererin (Seite 102)? Warum trägt sie einen Kittel?
2. Was machen die drei Kunden?
3. Hat die Kundin in der Mitte viel gekauft? Woher wissen Sie das?
4. Wo sieht man Körbe? Was sieht man darin?
5. Beschreiben Sie den Inhalt der Zeitschrift „Feste Feiern". Warum wird diese Zeitschrift in der Lebensmittelabteilung verkauft?

ZUR AUSFÜHRLICHEN DISKUSSION

1. Wann hat ein Lebensmittelgeschäft oder eine Lebensmittelabteilung viel Betrieb? Warum braucht man länger beim Einkaufen, wenn viel Betrieb herrscht?
2. Nachdem die Kassiererin Ihre Beträge zusammengezählt hat, bemerken Sie, daß Sie nicht genug Geld bei sich haben. Spielen Sie mit Ihrem Partner die Rollen von Kunden und Kassierer(in). Finden Sie eine Lösung!
3. Wie oft kaufen Sie im Lebensmittelgeschäft oder im Supermarkt ein? Welche Sachen kaufen Sie dort meistens?
4. Beschreiben Sie, warum Sie gern (oder nicht gern) im Lebensmittelgeschäft einkaufen.
5. Gehen Sie lieber allein oder mit jemandem zusammen einkaufen? Warum?

Man kann natürlich in Deutschland Lebensmittel auch in einem Supermarkt einkaufen.

1. Warum hängen Plakate in den Fenstern?
2. Befindet sich dieser Supermarkt in einer Stadt oder in einem Dorf? Woran erkennen Sie das?

3. Sie und Ihr(e) Kommiliton(in) haben 15 Mark bei sich. Kaufen Sie mit ihm oder ihr Lebensmittel für Abendessen und Frühstück ein. Was kaufen Sie?

Frühstückskarte _____

FRÜHSTÜCKSKARTE

KLEINES FRÜHSTÜCK

Portion Kaffee, Tee oder Schokolade, zwei Semmeln, Butter, Marmelade und
eine kleine Wurst—oder Käseplatte
DM 5,80

GROSSES FRÜHSTÜCK

Portion Kaffee, Tee oder Schokolade, ein Glas Orangensaft, ein weichgekochtes Ei,
zwei Semmeln, Butter, Marmelade und eine kleine Wurst—oder Käseplatte
DM 7,50

EXTRAS ZUM FRÜHSTÜCK

Glas Orangensaft	DM 2,50
Marmelade, Honig	DM -,80
Glas Milch	DM 1,20
Zwei Rühr-oder Spiegeleier mit Schinken	DM 4,50
Portion Butter	DM -,80
Ein weiches Ei	DM -,80
Becher Joghurt	DM 1,50
Geeiste Melone	DM 3,00
Semmeln, Brezeln, Schwarzbrot, Toast oder Vollkornbrot	DM -,50

10% Bedienung

WORTSCHATZ _____

der Becher, - *cup*
die Bedienung (der Service)
  service, table service
die Brezel, -n *pretzel*
die Butter *butter*
das Ei, -er *egg*
das Frühstück, -e *breakfast*

der Honig *honey*
der Joghurt *yogurt*
der Kaffee *coffee*
die Käseplatte, -n *cheese platter*
die Marmelade, -n *jam*
die Milch *milk*
der Orangensaft *orange juice*

105

die Portion, -en *portion (about 2½ cups)*
die Rühreier (*pl.*) *scrambled eggs*
der Schinken, - *smoked ham*
die Schokolade *(hot) chocolate*
das Schwarzbrot *black bread*
die Semmel, -n *small hard roll*

die Speisekarte, -n *menu*
die Spiegeleier (*pl.*) *fried eggs*
der Tee *tea*
der Toast *toast*
das Vollkornbrot *pumpernickel bread*

weichgekocht *soft boiled*
das Urteil, -e *judgment*

Im Restaurant „Rheinhof"

GAST: Herr Ober, die Frühstückskarte, bitte.
OBER: Haben sie schon gewählt? Was darf ich Ihnen bringen?
GAST: Können Sie mir etwas Gutes empfehlen?
OBER: Möchten Sie ein großes oder ein kleines Frühstück?
GAST: Nein, nichts großes. Ich nehme das kleine Frühstück zu 5 Mark 80.
OBER: Danke. Das kleine Frühstück. Zwei Semmeln, Butter, und Marmelade. Möchten Sie die Wurstplatte dazu?
GAST: Nein. Die Käseplatte, bitte.
OBER: Gern. Und möchten Sie lieber Kaffee, Tee oder Schokolade?
GAST: Kaffee, bitte.
OBER: Nehmen Sie Milch und Zucker zum Kaffee?
GAST: Nein, danke, ich trinke meinen Kaffee schwarz.
OBER: Hätten Sie gern Orangensaft dazu?
GAST: Haben Sie nichts anderes?
OBER: Wir haben auch Milch. Dazu kann ich Ihnen noch etwas Besonderes empfehlen—geeiste Melone.
GAST: Gut, ich verlasse mich ganz auf Ihr Urteil. Die Melone, bitte!

WORTSCHATZ

der Ober, - *waiter*
das Urteil, -e *judgment*
der Zucker *sugar*

empfehlen (empfiehlt), empfahl, empfohlen *to recommend*
sich verlassen (verläßt sich), verließ sich, sich verlassen auf (+ *acc.*) *to rely on*

wählen *to choose*

etwas Besonderes *something special*
etwas Gutes *something good*
etwas Kleines *something small*
etwas zum Kaffee nehmen *to take something in one's coffee*
nichts anderes *nothing else*

106

ZUM BESPRECHEN

1. Was würden Sie zum Frühstück bestellen? Warum?
2. Welches Frühstück kostet am meisten?
3. Wie lange soll man das Ei für Sie kochen?
4. Was essen Ihre Mutter oder Ihr Vater zum Frühstück?
5. Was nehmen Sie zum Kaffee? Zum Tee?
6. Was kostet das kleine Frühstück mit Bedienung?
7. Wieviel kostet das Frühstück, das der Gast bestellt hat?

ZUR AUSFÜHRLICHEN DISKUSSION

1. Spielen Sie die Rollen von Gast und Ober. Bestellen Sie ein Frühstück.
2. Wie unterscheidet sich das deutsche Frühstück vom amerikanischen Frühstück?
3. Wie spät frühstücken Sie gewöhnlich an Wochentagen? Am Samstag? Am Sonntag?
4. Was essen Sie normalerweise zum Frühstück?

Sind „Cornflakes" und „Special K" teurer oder billiger als in Amerika? (100 g = 3,5 Unzen; 1 Mark = ungefähr 50¢). In USA—7 ounces Special K = 57¢; 18 ounces Cornflakes = 83¢.

☙ ZUM MITTAGESSEN UND ABENDESSEN ❧

Vorspeisen (*Appetizers*)

Wurstsalat "nach Art des Hauses"	3,80
(*Sausage salad "home made"*)	
Tartar mit Ei und Butter	5,50
(*Steak tartar with egg and butter*)	
Krabbencocktail	6,80
(*Shrimp cocktail*)	
1 Portion Thunfisch mit Toast und Butter	4,30
(*Tuna fish with toast and butter*)	

Suppen (*Soups*)

Gulaschsuppe "hausgemacht"	2,80
(*Goulash soup "home made"*)	
Leberknödelsuppe	1,70
(*Liver dumpling soup*)	
Pfannkuchensuppe	1,50
(*Pancake (sliced) in clear soup*)	

Fisch (*Fish*)

Gebratene Forelle in Butter, Kartoffeln, Tomatensalat	16,-
(*Fried trout in butter, potatoes, tomato salad*)	
Schollenfilets in Bierteig gebacken, Tomatensauce, Butterkartoffeln, Kopfsalat	15,50
(*Filet of flounder baked in beer dough, tomato sauce, buttered potatoes, green salad*)	

Vom Grill und aus der Pfanne
(*From the grill and pan*)

Wiener Schnitzel mit Pommes frites	16,50
(*Wienerschnitzel with french fries*)	
Schweinebraten mit Kartoffelknödeln	14,50
(*Roast pork with potato dumplings*)	

Vom Spieß (*From the spit*)

1/2 Hähnchen vom Spieß mit Salatteller	11,-
(*1/2 Chicken with salad plate*)	

Nachspeisen (*Desserts*)

Apfelmus	1,70
(*Apple sauce*)	
Wiener Apfelstrudel	3,60
(*Viennese Applestrudel*)	
Gemischte Käseplatte	4,50
(*Mixed cheese platter*)	
Eiscreme nach Wahl	3,50
(*Choice of ice cream*)	
Obstsalat	5,-
(*Fresh fruit salad*)	

Getränke (*Beverages*)

Weißwein 1/4 1

Pfälzerwein	2,90
Bernkastler Riesling	3,30
Zeller Schwarze Katz	3,30

Rotwein 1/4 1

Beaujolais	3,30
Vin Rosé	3,30

Bier

Löwenbräu "Hell Export" vom Faß...0,2 1	-,90
Löwenbräu "Hell Export" vom Faß...0,5 1	2,40
Löwenbräu "Diätbier", Flasche 0,33 1	2,20

Alkoholfreie Getränke

Frischer Orangensaft	0,2 1	2,50
Apfelsaft	0,2 1	1,40
Coca Cola	0,2 1	1,50
Tasse Kaffee		1,80
Portion Kaffee		3,60
Tasse Kaffee, koffeinfrei		1,80
Portion Tee		3,60

ZUM BESPRECHEN

1. Welche Gerichte auf der Speisekarte findet man selten in Amerika?
2. Welche deutschen Speisen möchten Sie ausprobieren? Warum?
3. Essen Sie immer eine Vorspeise? Warum oder warum nicht?
4. Was sollten Sie bestellen, wenn Sie etwas mit wenig Kalorien essen wollen?
5. Welche Getränke soll man zu Fisch trinken? Was trinkt man zum Wiener Schnitzel oder Schweinebraten?
6. Sind die Preise für das Essen in Deutschland niedriger oder höher als in Amerika? (1 DM = ungefähr 50¢)

ZUR AUSFÜHRLICHEN DISKUSSION

1. Möchten Sie lieber in einem Restaurant oder zu Hause essen? Warum?
2. Spielen Sie die Rollen von Kellnerin und Gast mit einem Kollegen in der Klasse. Bestellen Sie ein vollständiges Abendessen.
3. Beschreiben Sie das beste Abendessen Ihres Lebens!
4. Wie oft essen Sie in einem Restaurant? Warum?
5. Was machen Sie, wenn Sie im Restaurant entdecken, daß Sie Ihr Geld vergessen haben?
6. Was machen Sie, wenn Sie ein Haar in Ihrer Gulaschsuppe finden?
7. Beschreiben Sie die Atmosphäre eines Restaurants, in dem Sie gern essen.

Speisekarte für Mittagessen in Wien

1. Können Sie die Speisekarte lesen?
2. Ist das Essen günstig oder teuer?
   (1 Schilling = ungefähr 6¢)

Die Imbißstube

1. Imbißstube an einer U-Bahn Haltestelle, München

2. Imbißstube im Hauptbahnhof

WORTSCHATZ

1.

die Bockwurst, ‥e *bockwurst*   die Currywurst, ‥e *curry sausage*
die Brühpolnisch *Polish sausage*   die Imbißstube, -n *snack bar*

der Kartoffelsalat   *potato salad*
der Lachs, -e   *salmon*
die Rindsbratwurst, ⁼e   *(beef) bratwurst*
das Sandwich, -es   *sandwich*
die Weißwurst, ⁼e   *white sausage*
das Wienerwürstl, - (Bavarian dialect)   *frankfurter*

2.

die Bratwurst, ⁼e   *fried sausage*
die Brotzeit (Bavarian & Austr. expression)   *between-meal snack*
der Leberkäs   *liver loaf*
die Pizza, -s   *pizza*

ZUM BESPRECHEN

1. Wodurch unterscheidet sich eine Imbißstube von einem Restaurant?
2. Wann ißt man in einer Imbißstube?
3. Wo findet man gewöhnlich Imbißstuben?
4. Welche amerikanischen Einflüsse sehen Sie auf den Bildern auf Seite 110?
5. Was machen die verschiedenen Kunden auf den Bildern?
6. Sie haben nur DM 5, - für Ihr Mittagessen. Was können Sie in der Imbißstube dafür kaufen?

McDonald's auch in Deutschland!

111

WORTSCHATZ

die Art, -en   *way, method*
die Cola, -s   *cola*
der Hamburger, -   *hamburger*
das Kakaogetränk, -e   *chocolate drink*
die Limo, -s   *lemon soda*
das Orangen-Kaltgetränk, -e *orangeade*
das Richtige   *the right thing*

bereit   *ready*
heiß   *hot*
preiswert   *worth the money*

eine Pause ein·legen   *to take a break*
Preise inklusive gesetzliche
  Mehrwertsteuer (MWSt.).   *Prices*
  include legal sales taxes.
zum Mitnehmen   *(food) to go, to take*
  out

ZUM BESPRECHEN

1. Essen Sie gern bei McDonald's? Warum oder warum nicht?
2. Finden Sie Unterschiede zwischen der deutschen und der amerikanischen Speisekarte bei McDonald's?
3. Ist McDonald's in Deutschland tatsächlich „preiswert" (1 DM = ungefähr 50¢)?
4. Welche Unterschiede finden Sie zwischen McDonald's und den Imbißstuben auf Seite 110?
5. Erklären Sie:
   „Leg mal eine Pause ein und komm zu McDonald's 'rein."

UNTERHALTSAMES ZUM LESEN UND BESPRECHEN

12

Die Werbung

WORTSCHATZ

die Anzeige, -n *advertisement*
der Benzindurst (*colloq.*) *gas "thirst"*
der Käfer, - *bug, VW*
die Reparatur, -en *repair*
die Unzuverlässigkeit *undependability, unreliability*
der Volkswagen, - *Volkswagen*
die Werbung *publicity, advertising*
die Werkstattrechnung, -en *repair shop bill*

sich ärgern über (+ *acc.*) *to get annoyed at*

chronisch *chronic*
dick *fat*
kaum *scarcely*
ständig *constantly*
wirtschaftlich *economical*
zuverlässig *dependable*

Mensch ärgere dich nicht.
Es gibt doch den Käfer.

Der Käfer ärgert Sie nicht mit ständigen Reparaturen, Werkstattrechnungen, dicken Versicherungsprämien, großem Benzindurst und chronischer Unzuverlässigkeit. Er ist zuverlässig und wirtschaftlich wie kaum ein zweites Auto.

ZUM BESPRECHEN ————————————————————————————

1. Warum sollte sich der Mensch über den Käfer nicht ärgern?
2. Warum müßte die Anzeige jetzt heißen: „Es *gab* doch den Käfer?"

Ein Katertag ist ein verlorener Tag.

Alka-Seltzer®hilft gegen Katergefühl. Denn es wirkt auf Kopf und Magen zugleich. Und es hilft besonders schnell, weil es in Wasser gelöst eingenommen wird. Miles GmbH, Frankfurt.

WORTSCHATZ

der Kater, - *hangover; tom cat*
das Katergefühl, -e *hungover feeling*
der Kopf, ⁒ *head*
der Magen, ⁒ *stomach*
das Produkt, -e *product*

ein·nehmen (nimmt ein), nahm ein,
  eingenommen *to take (medicine)*
fest·stellen *to determine*

lösen *to solve, dissolve*
wirken auf (+ acc.) *to affect, act on*

anschließend *afterwards*
jeweils *respectively*
zugleich *at the same time*

Mir ist schlecht. *I feel ill.*

ZUM BESPRECHEN

1. Haben Sie je einen Kater gehabt? Wann? Beschreiben Sie die Umstände!
2. Warum ist ein Katertag ein verlorener Tag?
3. Nehmen Sie manchmal Alka-Seltzer ein, wenn Ihnen schlecht ist? Warum oder warum nicht?

ZUR AUSFÜHRLICHEN DISKUSSION

116

1. Bringen Sie eine Anzeige aus einer Zeitung in die Klasse mit. Versuchen Sie, Ihren Klassenkameraden das Produkt zu verkaufen. Beantworten Sie jeweils die Fragen, die jedes Klassenmitglied stellt. Stellen Sie anschließend fest, wie viele Studenten Ihr Produkt kaufen würden.
2. Schreiben Sie Ihre eigene Anzeige, und bringen Sie sie in die Klasse mit.

Der Cartoon

WORTSCHATZ

die Bombe, -n *bomb*
der Cartoon, -s *cartoon*
die Moral *moral*
der Zünder, - *fuse*

weg·laufen (läuft weg), lief weg, ist
  weggelaufen *to run away*
explodieren; detonieren *to explode,*
  detonate

an·zünden *to light, ignite*
brennen, brannte, gebrannt *to burn*
schütteln *to shake*

neugierig *curious*
unsicher *uncertain*

ZUM BESPRECHEN

117

1. Erzählen Sie, was in jeder Szene dieses Cartoons passiert.
2. Hat dieser kleine Cartoon eine Moral?

Das Märchen

Das kleine Mädchen und der Wolf

James Thurber

Eines Nachmittages saß ein großer Wolf in einem finsteren Wald und wartete darauf, daß ein kleines Mädchen mit einem Korb voller Lebensmittel für ihre Großmutter des Weges käme. Endlich kam auch ein kleines Mädchen des Weges, und sie trug einen Korb voller Lebensmittel. „Bringst du den Korb zu deiner Großmutter?" fragte der Wolf. Das kleine Mädchen sagte ja, und nun erkundigte sich der Wolf, wo die Großmutter wohne. Das kleine Mädchen gab ihm Auskunft, und der Wolf verschwand im Wald.

Als das kleine Mädchen das Haus ihrer Großmutter betrat, sah sie, daß jemand im Bett lag, der ein Nachthemd und eine Nachthaube trug. Sie war noch keine drei Schritte auf das Bett zugegangen, da merkte sie, daß es nicht ihre Großmutter war, sondern der Wolf, denn selbst in einer Nachthaube sieht ein Wolf einer Großmutter nicht ähnlicher als der Metro-Goldwyn-Meyer-Löwe dem Präsidenten der Vereinigten Staaten. Also nahm das kleine Mädchen einen Browning aus ihrem Korb und schoß den Wolf tot.

Moral: Es ist heutzutage nicht mehr so leicht wie früher, kleinen Mädchen etwas vorzumachen.

WORTSCHATZ

die Nachthaube, -n *sleeping bonnet*

betreten (betritt), betrat, betreten *to enter*

sich erkundigen *to inquire*

schießen, schoß, geschossen *to shoot*

verschwinden, verschwand, ist

verschwunden *to disappear*

etwas vor·machen (+ *dat. with people*) *to take in, fool*

ähnlich *similar*

finster *dark*

früher *formerly*

ZUM BESPRECHEN

1. Wo wartete der große Wolf? Auf wen wartete er?
2. Wieso scheint das Mädchen zuerst naiv zu sein?
3. Was merkte das kleine Mädchen, als es auf das Bett zuging?
4. Wie unterscheidet sich der Schluß dieses Märchens von Grimms „Rotkäppchen"?
5. Erklären Sie die Moral des Märchens. Stimmt die Moral nur für Mädchen oder auch für Jungen?

Zungenbrecher

Lesen Sie die folgenden Sätze so schnell wie möglich vor!

1. Fischers Fritze fischte frische Fische, frische Fische fischte Fischers Fritze.
2. Wir Wiener Wäschweiber wollten weiße Wäsche waschen, wenn wir wüßten, wo weiches, warmes Wasser wäre.
3. Ach, ich bin so recht und schlecht einer echten Ächtung entwichen.
4. Brautkleid bleibt Brautkleid.

   Blaukraut bleibt Blaukraut.
5. In Ulm, um Ulm und um Ulm herum.
6. Zwischen zwei Zwetschgenzweigen zwitschern zwei Zwitscherschwalben.
7. Bierbrauer braut Braunbier.
8. Es saßen zwei zischende Schlangen zwischen zwei spitzigen Steinen und zischten dazwischen.
9. Schneiders Schere schneidet scharf, scharf schneidet Schneiders Schere.
10. Niemand schneidet mit dem Buttermesser als die Mutter besser.
11. Wer immer angelt, der nimmer mangelt.
12. Wenn mancher Mann wüßte, wer mancher Mann wär', gäb mancher Mann manchem Mann manchmal mehr Ehr'.

Der Witz

Witz der Woche

Ein Tourist fragt den Bürgermeister des Dorfes: „Ist das Klima hier gesund?"
„Und ob", versichert der Bürgermeister, „wir mußten unseren ältesten Einwohner vergiften, um endlich den Friedhof einweihen zu können."

WORTSCHATZ

der Bürgermeister, - *mayor*
der Einwohner, - *resident*
der Friedhof, ⸚e *cemetery*
das Klima, -ta *climate*

ein·weihen *to dedicate*
vergiften *to poison*
versichern *to assure*

Und ob! *And how!*

119

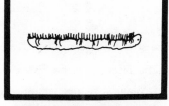

Schlafender Tausendfüßler!

Erzählen Sie der Klasse Ihren eignen „Witz der Woche"!

Witz der Woche

Sprichwörter

1. Aller Anfang ist schwer.
2. Morgenstund hat Gold im Mund.
3. Kleider machen Leute.
4. Übung macht den Meister.
5. Jeder ist seines Glückes Schmied.
6. Wie man sich bettet, so liegt man.
7. Allen Menschen recht getan, ist eine Kunst, die niemand kann.
8. Ein Unglück kommt selten allein.
9. Morgen, morgen nur nicht heute, sagen alle faulen Leute.
10. Wenn die Katze fort ist, tanzen die Mäuse.
11. Der Apfel fällt nicht weit vom Stamm.
12. Reden ist Silber, Schweigen ist Gold.
13. Es ist noch kein Meister vom Himmel gefallen.

WORTSCHATZ

der Anfang, ⸚e   *beginning*
die Kunst, ⸚e   *art*
der Schmied, -e   *(black)smith*
das Schweigen   *silence*
das Unglück   *misfortune*

erläutern   *to illustrate*

anhand von   *by means of*
recht tun (+ *dat.*)   *to please*

ZUM BESPRECHEN

120

1. Erklären Sie jedes Sprichwort.
2. Wählen Sie ein Sprichwort aus und erläutern Sie es anhand eines Beispiels aus Ihrem Leben.

Das Gedicht

1. Aus Glas

Josef Guggenmos

Manchmal denke ich mir irgendwas.
Und zum Spaß
denke ich mir jetzt, ich bin aus Glas.

Alle Leute, die da auf der Straße gehen
bleiben stehen,
um einander durch mich anzusehen.

Und die vielen andern Kinder schrein:
,,Ei, wie fein!
Ich, ich, ich will auch durchsichtig sein!''

Doch ein Lümmel stößt mich in den Rücken.
Ich fall' hin . . .
Klirr, da liege ich in tausend Stücken.

Ach, ich bleibe lieber, wie ich bin!

WORTSCHATZ

der Lümmel, - *lout, ruffian, boor*
der Rücken, - *back*
das Stück, -e *piece*

bewundern *to admire*
sich denken, dachte sich, sich gedacht
 (*dat.*) *to think to oneself*
hin·fallen (fällt hin), fiel hin, ist
 hingefallen *to fall down*
reagieren auf (+ *acc.*) *to react to*
schreien, schrie, geschrien *to cry,
 scream*

stehen·bleiben, blieb stehen, ist
 stehengeblieben *to stop*
stoßen (stößt), stieß, gestoßen *to
 push, shove*

durchsichtig *transparent*
einander *one another*
irgendwas *something*
klirr! *smash!*

im Zusammenhang mit *in connection
 with*
zum Spaß *for fun*

ZUM BESPRECHEN

1. Warum will dieses Kind aus Glas sein?
2. Wie reagieren die Leute und die anderen Kinder? Warum?
3. Was tut der Lümmel? Haben Sie jemals in Ihrem Leben einen Lümmel kennengelernt? Erzählen Sie etwas darüber!
4. Versuchen Sie, die Moral dieses Gedichts zu erklären. Glauben Sie, man sollte lieber bleiben, wie man ist?
5. Erklären Sie im Zusammenhang mit diesem Gedicht das Sprichwort ,,Glück und Glas, wie leicht bricht das''.

121

2. Kinderhände

Hans Baumann

Ein Holländerkind,
ein Negerkind,
ein Chinesenkind
drückten beim Spielen die Hände in Lehm.
Nun geh hin und sag, welche Hand ist von wem!

WORTSCHATZ

die Hand, ⸚e *hand*   drücken   *to press*
der Lehm   *mud, clay*
der Sinn   *sense*   beim Spielen   *at play*

ZUM BESPRECHEN

1. Warum sind Kinder besonders geeignet als Thema dieses Gedichts?
2. Warum wählt der Dichter gerade diese drei Kinder aus?
3. Was kann man im Lehm nicht mehr erkennen?
4. Erklären Sie den Sinn dieses Gedichts.

DIE TANKSTELLE DAS AUTO

13

DAS AUTO

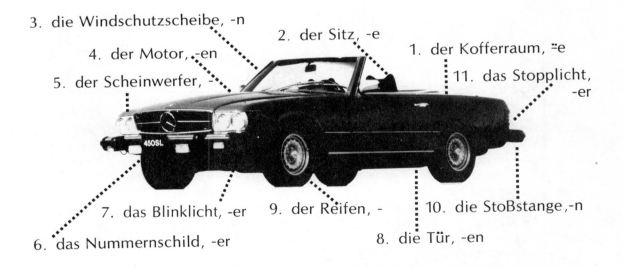

3. die Windschutzscheibe, -n

2. der Sitz, -e

1. der Kofferraum, ̈e

4. der Motor, -en

11. das Stopplicht, -er

5. der Scheinwerfer, -

7. das Blinklicht, -er

9. der Reifen, -

10. die Stoßstange, -n

6. das Nummernschild, -er

8. die Tür, -en

WORTSCHATZ

das Auto, -s; der Wagen, -
  automobile
das Fahrzeug, -e *motor vehicle*
das Kabriolett, -s *convertible*
der Kastenwagen, - *van*
der Kleinlaster, - *pick-up truck*
der Kombiwagen, - *station wagon*
die Limousine, -n *sedan*
der Rennfahrer, - *race car driver*
der Sportwagen, - *sports car*
der Teil, -e *part (auto)*
der Typ, -en *model, type*

beladen (belädt), belud, beladen *to
load*

bezeichnen *to designate, characterize*
entladen (entlädt), entlud,
 entladen *to unload*

bequem *comfortable*
eng *narrow, cramped*
geräumig *roomy, spacious*
praktisch *practical*
schnell *fast*
sportlich *sporty*

ZUR BESPRECHUNG

1. Bezeichnen Sie jeden Fahrzeugtyp auf den Fotos.
2. Für welche Zwecke sind die folgenden Autotypen am besten geeignet?
   a) der Sportwagen
   b) der Kleinlaster
   c) der Kombiwagen
   d) die Limousine
3. Welchen Fahrzeugtyp ziehen Sie vor? Warum?
4. Beschreiben Sie die Funktionen der folgenden Autoteile.
   a) das Stopplicht
   b) das Blinklicht
   c) der Motor
   d) der Kofferraum
   e) der Scheinwerfer
   f) der Sitz
   g) die Windschutzscheibe

ZUR BESPRECHUNG

1. Was für einen Wagen fährt der Rennfahrer?
2. Warum lächeln die Mädchen?
3. Was sagen die Mädchen zu dem Fahrer?
   Was antwortet der Mann?
4. Würden Sie so einen Wagen kaufen? Warum oder warum nicht?

125

AUTOANZEIGEN

VW GOLF, Baujahr 77, automatisches Getriebe, 4 Türen, Garagenwagen, 58000 km, Radio, getönte Scheiben, sehr gepflegt. Günstig zu verkaufen. Tel. 759486 ab Montag.

VW KÄFER 1300, feuerrot, Baujahr 70, mit Motorschaden, DM 300. Liebhaberstück, Tel. 08145 ab 18 Uhr.

OPEL REKORD, Baujahr 75, 97 PS, Stahlgürtelreifen, 68000 km, rostfrei, viele Extras, guter Zustand. TÜV fällig. Tel. 789430.

BMW 2002, Baujahr 73, Blechschaden, Motor einwandfrei, dunkelblau, neue Kupplung und Bremsen, Radio, von Privat zu verkaufen. DM 2400.

VW CABRIO, Baujahr 77, signalorange, Motor überholt, technisch und optisch sehr guter Zustand, Winterreifen, Kassettenradio. TÜV neu. DM 10700. Tel. 475837 ab Sonntag abend.

MERCEDES BENZ 450 SLC, Baujahr 79, unfallfrei, automatisches Schiebedach, Automatik, Ledersitze, Stereo-Kassette, Zentralverriegelung, silber-metallic, elektrische Fenster und Antenne, Servolenkung, Scheinwerferwischer, nur 5000 km.
Zu verkaufen oder zu leasen. Nachmittags 089/675820.

PORSCHE CARRERA TARGA TURBO,
Baujahr 78, 5 Gang Schaltung, Heckspoiler, Nebelscheinwerfer, Klimaanlage, Skiträger, heizbare Heckscheibe, elektrischer Spiegel, Stereo-Kasette, Topzustand. Kaufen Sie auf Raten. Nur DM 72000. Tel.: 089/679482

MOTORRAD: BMW R100RS,
Baujahr 79, wie neu, alles poliert und verchromt. Festpreis 11000 DM. Tutzinger Straße 2a.

FORD TRANSIT KASTENWAGEN, 77, 1 ¾ Tonne, optisch und technisch wie neu, DM 9900, – und 11% Mehrwertsteuer. Tel. 414407.

VW-CAMPINGBUS, 79, vollausgestattet, 4 Schlafplätze mit Toilettenraum. 16000 DM. 945874.

WORTSCHATZ

die Antenne, -n *antenna*
die Anzeige, -n *advertisement*
das automatische Getriebe, - *automatic transmission*
die Ausstattung, -en *equipment*
das Baujahr, -e *year of construction*
die Betriebskosten (*pl.*) *maintenance expenses*
die Bremse, -n *brake*
das Fenster, - *window*
der Gang, ⁻e *gear*

die Garantie, -n *guarantee, warranty*
der Händler, - *dealer*
die Klimaanlage, -n *air conditioning*
die Kupplung, -en *clutch*
der Ledersitz, -e *leather seat*
das Liebhaberstück, -e *collector's item*
die Mehrwertsteuer, -n *German sales tax*
das Motorrad, ⁻er *motorcycle*
die Servolenkung, -en *power steering*

126

der Skiträger, - *ski rack*
der Spiegel, - *mirror*
die Tür, -en *door*
der TÜV (Technischer
Überwachungsverein) *technical*
inspection association*
der Unfall, ⸚e *accident*
der Volkswagen, - *Volkswagen (all*
makes of cars are masculine in
gender)
der Winterreifen, - *snow tire*

sich an·schnallen *to buckle one's*
seatbelt
kaufen *to buy*
pflegen *to care for*
polieren *to polish*
schalten *to shift*
verkaufen *to sell*
vor·schreiben, schrieb vor,
vorgeschrieben *to prescribe, require*

automatisch *automatic*
dunkelblau *dark blue*
einwandfrei *mint condition*
fällig *due*
feuerrot *fire engine red*
gebraucht *used*
gepflegt *well cared for*
mechanisch *mechanical(ly)*
nachmittags *afternoons*
optisch *optically*
rostfrei *rust-free*
silber-metallic *metallic silver*
technisch *technical(ly)*
unfallfrei *free of accidents*
verchromt *chromed*

achten auf (+ acc.) *to pay attention to*
in Zahlung geben *to trade in*

ZUM BESPRECHEN

1. Kaufen Sie lieber einen neuen oder einen gebrauchten Wagen? Warum?
2. Worauf sollten Sie achten, wenn Sie einen Gebrauchtwagen kaufen?
3. Welche Ausstattung möchten Sie in Ihrem Wagen haben? Warum?
4. Beschreiben Sie das Auto, das Ihre Familie besitzt oder das Sie selber besitzen.
5. Schnallen Sie sich an, wenn Sie fahren? Warum ist es wichtig, sich immer anzuschnallen?
6. Alle zwei Jahre muß ein deutsches Fahrzeug vom TÜV überprüft werden. Ist auch in Ihrem Staat eine technische Überprüfung vorgeschrieben? Erklären Sie die Vorteile des TÜVs. Was sind einige Nachteile?
7. Nennen Sie die Vor- und Nachteile eines Motorrads.
8. Beschreiben Sie Ihrem Partner in der Klasse Ihr Traumauto.
9. Warum ist es nicht immer vorteilhaft, ein Auto auf Raten zu kaufen?
10. Wenn Sie Ihr Auto verkaufen wollen, ist es dann besser, eine Anzeige in die Zeitung zu setzen oder Ihr Auto bei einem Händler in Zahlung zu geben?

ZUR AUSFÜHRLICHEN DISKUSSION

1. Sehen Sie sich die Autoanzeigen an. Spielen Sie die Rollen von Käufer(in) und Verkäufer(in). Stellen Sie dem Verkäufer so viele Fragen wie möglich über seinen Wagen.
2. Beschreiben Sie die Unterschiede zwischen amerikanischen und europäischen Autos.
3. Was muß man tun, um ein guter Autofahrer zu sein?
4. Welches sind die Betriebskosten eines Autos?

127

---

* German motor vehicles must undergo a rigorous technical inspection every two years

der Gebrauchtwagen

WORTSCHATZ

die Anzahlung, -en *down payment*
der Gastarbeiter, - *foreign worker**
der Gebrauchtwagen, - *used car*
der Privatbesitzer *private owner*
die Rate, -n *installment payment*

garantieren *to guarantee, warrant*

leicht *easy*

128

* Ausländische Arbeitnehmer (ungefähr 2 Millionen in Deutschland), die aus der Türkei, Griechenland, Jugoslawien, Italien oder Spanien kommen. Sie tun die schmutzigsten Arbeiten, bekommen meistens nur die schlechtesten Wohnungen und bleiben überwiegend Außenseiter der Gesellschaft. Trotzdem haben die Gastarbeiter einen höheren Lebensstandard als viele Arme in den USA.

ZUM BESPRECHEN

1. Für wie lange gibt der Autohändler Garantie für jedes Auto?
2. Warum scheint es einfach zu sein, bei diesem Autohändler ein Auto zu kaufen?
3. Kaufen Sie lieber einen Wagen bei einem Autohändler oder von einem Privatbesitzer? Warum?
4. Warum steht auf dem Schild: „Auch für Gastarbeiter?"

die Parkuhr

WORTSCHATZ

die Minute, -n *minute*
der Parkplatz, ⁼e *parking place*
die Parkuhr, -en *parking meter*
der Pfennig, -e *pfennig (100 pfennige = 1 Mark)*

der Werktag, -e *week day*

ein·werfen (wirft ein), warf ein, eingeworfen *to deposit, insert*
parken *to park*

ZUM BESPRECHEN

1. Wie lange darf man an dieser Parkuhr parken?
2. Wieviel kostet das Parken?
3. An welchen Tagen und in welcher Zeit muß man Geld in die Parkuhr einwerfen?

WORTSCHATZ

das Fahrrad, ⸚er *bicycle*   der Strafzettel, - *ticket, summons*
die Politesse, -n *meter maid*
die Strafe, -n *penalty, fine*   beobachten *to observe*

ZUM BESPRECHEN

1. Was tut die Politesse auf dem Bild? Warum?
2. Warum beobachtet der Mann links die Szene? Gebrauchen Sie viel Phantasie bei Ihrer Beschreibung.
3. Wieviel müssen Sie in Ihrer Stadt für einen Strafzettel bezahlen?
4. Haben Sie je einen Strafzettel bekommen? Erzählen Sie kurz davon!

WORTSCHATZ

der Helm, -e *helmet* sich streiten, stritt sich, sich
die Pistole, -n *pistol, gun* gestritten *to quarrel, argue*

ZUM BESPRECHEN

1. Beschreiben Sie diese Szene!
2. Was trägt der Polizist? Warum?
3. Streiten sich die Dame und der Polizist, oder sprechen sie freundlich miteinander?
4. Warum steht der Kofferraum des Autos offen?

131

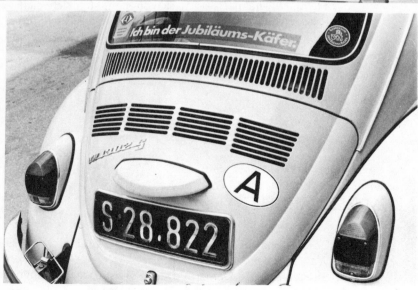

Das Nummernschild

Deutsche Kraftfahrzeug-Kennzeichen

A	Augsburg		KG	Bad Kissingen
AH	Ahaus		LH	Lüdinghausen
B	Berlin		MA	Mannheim
BH	Buhl		MM	Memmingen
CAS	Castrop-Rauxel		NAB	Nabburg
CO	Coburg		OB	Oberhausen Rheinland
DA	Darmstadt		PA	Passau
DI	Dieburg		RA	Rastatt
E	Essen		RW	Rottweil
EU	Euskirchen		S	Stuttgart
FD	Fulda		STO	Stockach Baden
FU	Fürth Bayern		TÜ	Tübingen
GD	Schwäbisch-Gmünd		UL	Ulm Donau
HA	Hagen Westfalen		VK	Völklingen
IS	Iserlohn		W	Wuppertal
K	Köln		ZW	Zweibrücken

1. Was bedeuten Ⓓ Ⓕ ⒸⒽ Ⓐ ?

2. Warum muß jedes Auto ein Nummernschild haben?

3. Benennen Sie jedes Automodell.

4. Welches dieser Automodelle haben Sie schon in Amerika gesehen?

Die Tankstelle

1.

2.

3.

134

WORTSCHATZ

die Art, -en *type, kind*
der Auspuff, -e *exhaust*
der Autoverleih, -e *auto rental agency*
das Auto-Zubehör *auto-accessory*
die Batterie, -n *battery*
die Bedienung *service*
das Benzin *gasoline*
der Dienst, -e *service*
die Gallone, -n *gallon*
das Kraftfahrzeug (KFZ), -e *motor vehicle*
der Liter, - *liter*
der Motor, -en *engine*
das Öl, -e *oil*
der Ölwechsel, - *oil change*
die Panne, -n *breakdown (auto)*
die Reifenpanne, -n *flat tire*
der Reifen, - *tire*
die Reparatur, -en *repair*
die Schnellwäsche, -n *quick wash*
die Selbstbedienung *self-service*
der Stoßdämpfer, - *shock-absorber*
der Tank, -s *tank*
der Tankwart, -e *service station attendant*
die Tankstelle, -n *gas station*
die Umwelt *environment*

der Volkswagen (VW), - *VW*
die Windschutzscheibe, -n *windshield*
die Zapfsäule, -n *gas pump*

an·bieten, bot an, angeboten *to offer*
erfahren (erfährt), erfuhr, erfahren *to learn, find out*
mieten *to rent*
prüfen *to test*
reparieren *to repair*
schützen *to protect*
steigern *to increase*
tanken *to get gasoline, fill up*
verleihen, verlieh, verliehen *to rent out*
wechseln *to change*

durchgehend *continuously*
samstags *Saturdays*
sofort *immediately*
täglich *daily*

den Motor ab·stellen *to turn off the engine*
den Motor an·lassen *to start the engine*
sich verfahren *to get lost (travelling)*

135

ZUM BESPRECHEN

1. Was tut der Mann auf dem ersten Foto (Seite 134)? Was für einen Wagen hat er?
2. Was kann man an der Esso-Tankstelle außer Benzin noch bekommen?
3. Was macht der Mann, nachdem der Tank voll ist?
4. Woher weiß man, wieviel man für das Benzin bezahlen muß?
5. Welche Dienste bietet die Fina-Tankstelle (*Foto 3*) an?
6. Wie lang ist die Fina-Tankstelle täglich geöffnet?
7. Was kann man im „Auto-Shop" kaufen?
8. Wie weiß man, daß der Auspuff an einem Auto kaputt ist?
9. Was macht man, wenn man eine Reifenpanne hat?
10. Wie unterscheidet sich eine Tankstelle mit Bedienung von einer Tankstelle mit Selbstbedienung?
11. Weshalb geht man zu einem Autoverleih? Welche Vor- und Nachteile hat es, einen Wagen zu mieten?
12. Warum hat eine Tankstelle drei Arten Benzin (*Foto 2*)?
13. Benzin kostet DM -,86⁹, -,90⁹, -,88⁹ *pro Liter* (3,8 Liter = 1 Gallone). Kostet Benzin in Deutschland also mehr oder weniger als in Amerika?
14. Ein VW hat einen 40-Liter Tank. Wieviel kostet es, vollzutanken?

ZUR AUSFÜHRLICHEN DISKUSSION

1. Was können Sie tun, wenn Sie sich mit dem Auto verfahren haben?
2. Beschreiben Sie Ihren Klassenkameraden eine Autopanne, die Sie oder Ihre Familie gehabt haben. Was haben Sie gemacht?
3. Was tun Sie, wenn der Motor nicht anspringt?
4. Erklären Sie die Aufschrift „Umwelt schützen. Bitte Motor abstellen!"
5. Sprechen Sie über die steigenden Benzinpreise. Was würde in Amerika geschehen, wenn Benzin mehr als $1.60 pro Gallone (wie in Deutschland) kosten würde?

STELLENANGEBOTE

14

Stellenangebote/Männlich und Weiblich

1.

Für unsere Geschäfte auf dem Flughafen Frankfurt suchen wir tüchtige und zuverlässige

VERKÄUFER UND VERKÄUFERINNEN

mit englischen Sprachkenntnissen.

Unsere Geschäfte sind täglich von 7–21 Uhr geöffnet. Auch wenn Sie nur an Wochenenden arbeiten möchten, können Sie bei uns Beschäftigung finden.

Bitte setzen Sie sich schriftlich oder telefonisch mit uns in Verbindung.

FLUGHAFEN FRANKFURT GmbH, Knorrstraße 142, 6 Frankfurt 71, tel. 061-516836

WORTSCHATZ

die Beschäftigung, -en *employment*
das Geschäft, -e *store, business*
der Flughafen, ⸗ *airport*
die Sprachkenntnisse (*pl.*) *knowledge of a language*
das Stellenangebot, -e *job advertisement*
das Wochenende, -n *weekend*

arbeiten *to work*
finden, fand, gefunden *to find*

schriftlich *in writing*
telefonisch *by telephone*
tüchtig *qualified, skilled*

sich in Verbindung setzen (mit) *to contact*

137

2.

BONANZA Jeans-Store
am Rindermarkt

sucht Verkäufer(innen)

für ganz- und halbtags. Unser Profi-Team ist nichts für Drückeberger! Aber wenn Sie flink sind, können Sie viel Erfolg und
einen sicheren Arbeitsplatz bei uns haben. Sie werden dann auch
sehr gut bezahlt (Urlaubsgeld, Weihnachtsgeld).

Bitte rufen Sie uns an. Tel. 2608553

WORTSCHATZ

der Arbeitsplatz, -̈e *job*
der Drückeberger, - *work-shirker*
der Erfolg, -e *success*
die Jeans (*pl.*) *jeans*
der Profi, -s *professional*
das Team, -s *team*
das Urlaubsgeld *vacation money*
das Weihnachtsgeld *Christmas money*

an·rufen, rief an, angerufen *to call up,
    telephone*
bezahlen *to pay*

flink *quick, alert*
ganztags *full days*
halbtags *half days*

3.

Gymnasium in München sucht für das nächste Schuljahr

DEUTSCHLEHRER(IN) mit STAATSEXAMEN

Moderne Schule, angenehmer Kollegenkreis, Sport-
möglichkeiten. Bewerbungen an: Städtisches Willi-Graf-
Gymnasium, Borschtallee 26, 8000 München 40.

WORTSCHATZ

die Bewerbung, -en *application*
das Gymnasium, -ien *secondary
    school (for pupils 10–19 years old
    who are preparing for university
    study)*
der Kollege, -n, -n *colleague (male)*
der Kollegenkreis, -e *circle of
    colleagues, faculty*

die Kollegin, -nen *colleague (female)*
die Möglichkeit, -en *possibility*
das Schuljahr, -e *school year*

angenehm *pleasant*
nächst *next*

138

4.

SIEMENS

Sind Sie einsatzfreudig und verantwortungsbewußt?
Sind Sie an selbständiges Arbeiten gewöhnt?

Wir bieten Ihnen eine interessante Stellung als

COBOL-Programmierer(in)

für Software und

ASSEMBLER-Programmierer(in)

Sie müssen in der Lage sein, unsere Programme weiter
zu entwickeln und neue Programme dazu zu erstellen.
Sind Sie interessiert? Dann schreiben Sie bitte an HB
159, unsere Zentrale Personalabteilung, 7600 Offenburg,
Wittelsbacherplatz 2.

WORTSCHATZ

der Computer, - *computer*
die Personalabteilung, -en *personnel department*
das Programm, -e *program*
der Programmierer, - *programmer (male)*
die Programmiererin, -nen *programmer (female)*
die Stellung, -en *job*

bieten, bot, geboten *to offer*

entwickeln *to develop*
erstellen *to make, set up*

einsatzfreudig *happy to initiate*
verantwortungsbewußt *responsible*
weiter *further*

an etwas (*acc.*) gewöhnt sein *to be accustomed to something*
in der Lage sein *to be capable, to be in a postion*

5.

Suche ab sofort für exklusive Diskothek im Raum Nürn-
berg qualifizierten

DISCJOCKEY

Tel. ab 20 Uhr 09122/76676, tagsüber 09560/351

WORTSCHATZ

der Discjockey, -s *disk jockey*
die Diskothek, -en *discothèque*

exklusiv *exclusive*
qualifiziert *qualified*

tagsüber *in the daytime*

ab sofort *immediately*
im Raum *in the area*

139

6.

> NACHTPORTIER UND HAUSMÄDCHEN für 3 oder 4
> Tage in der Woche und
>
> FRAU FÜR DIE KÜCHE
>
> eventuell auch nachmittags oder abends gesucht

WORTSCHATZ

das Hausmädchen, - *maid*
die Küche, -n *kitchen*
der Nachtportier, -s *night porter*

abends *in the evening*

eventuell *probably, possibly*
nachmittags *in the afternoon*

in der Woche *per week, every week*

7.

> TAXIFAHRER(INNEN)
> für Neuwagen (Mercedes) mit Lenkhilfe,
> gesucht.
> Tel. 478513

WORTSCHATZ

die Lenkhilfe *power steering*
das Taxi, -s *taxicab*
der Taxifahrer, - *taxi driver (male)*

die Taxifahrerin, -nen *taxi driver*
   (female)

8.

> Job für junge Leute! Wer will wie ich *DM 1000, - und
> mehr* im Monat
> verdienen? Ab 17 Uhr, Pkw erforderlich. Tel. 089/775844

WORTSCHATZ

der Job, -s *job*
der Pkw (Personenkraftwagen), -
   passenger car

erforderlich *required*

9.

Als einer der führenden MERCEDES Händler in Karlsruhe suchen wir

1 Automobil-Juniorverkäufer

Wir erwarten Zielstrebigkeit, Zuverlässigkeit, Einsatzfreude und Verhandlungsgeschick.

Erfahrenen Herren geben wir den Vorzug; jedoch auch unerfahrenen Bewerbern, die sich für das anspruchsvolle Geschäft des Automobilverkäufers eignen, geben wir eine Chance.

Bitte richten Sie Ihre schriftliche Bewerbung mit Lebenslauf an:

Autohaus Karlsruhe GmbH
Straßburger Allee 16
7500 Karlsruhe

WORTSCHATZ

der Bewerber, - *applicant*
die Einsatzfreude *initiative*
der Händler, - *dealer*
der Lebenslauf, ⁼e *resumé*
das Verhandlungsgeschick *skill in negotiation*
die Zielstrebigkeit *resoluteness*

sich eignen (für) *to be suitable (for)*
erwarten *to expect*

richten an (+ acc.) *to direct to*

anspruchsvoll *exacting, demanding*
erfahren *experienced*
führend *leading*
unerfahren *inexperienced*

jemandem den Vorzug geben *to give someone preference*

10.

1 BÄCKER
1 KONDITOR
für sofort gesucht. Beste Bezahlung,
eventuell Kost und Einzelzimmer im Hause.

Bäckerei/Konditorei W. Reif, Drachenseestr. 5
A-1110 Wien Tel. 7894930

WORTSCHATZ

der Bäcker, - *baker*
die Bäckerei, -en *bakery*
die Bezahlung *pay*
das Einzelzimmer, - *single room*
der Konditor, -en *pastry-baker*

die Konditorei, -en *café with pastries*
die Kost *food, board*

141

11.

> *Automechaniker oder Tankwart gesucht.* Deutsch-sprachig mit Autokenntnissen. Für SHELL-Selbstbe-dienungs-Tankstelle, Landsberger Str. 543, 4000 Düs-seldorf. Telefon: 574950

WORTSCHATZ

die Autokenntnisse (*pl.*) *knowledge of cars*
der Automechaniker, - *auto mechanic*
der Tankwart, -e *gas station attendant*
die Selbstbedienung *self-service*

reparieren *to repair*

deutschsprachig *German-speaking*

12.

> Zuverlässiger, freundlicher
>
> HAUSMEISTER
>
> für Eigentumswohnungen in Hamburg. Betreuung und Reinigung. Ab sofort gesucht. Gehalt DM 2900,—. Ver-billigte 3-Zimmer-Wohnung.
>
> Bewerbungen an: G. Häusl, Alndorferstraße 50, 2 Hamburg 70 Telefon 495083

WORTSCHATZ

die Betreuung *care and control*
die Eigentumswohnung, -en *condominium*
das Gehalt, ⸚er *salary*
der Hausmeister, - *caretaker, janitor*

die Pflicht, -en *duty*
die Reinigung *cleaning*
die Wohnung, -en *apartment*

verbilligt *reduced in price*

13.

Ihre Chance! Werden Sie

Fremdsprachen-Sekretärin,

die Freude hat, mitzudenken und selbständig zu arbeiten. Englisch perfekt in Wort und Schrift mit erstklassiger Berufserfahrung.

Wir bieten eine Dauerstellung in modernem Büro in der City. Gehalt nach Vereinbarung.

Bewerbungen mit handgeschriebenem Lebenslauf und Lichtbild an

Chemische Fabrik GmbH
Donaustaufer Str. 943
8400 Regensburg

WORTSCHATZ

die Berufserfahrung, -en *occupational experience*
das Büro, -s *office*
die City, -s *center city*
die Dauerstellung, -en *long-term position*
die Fremdsprache, -n *foreign language*
die Freude, -n *joy*
das Lichtbild, -er *photograph*

die Schrift, -en *writing, handwriting*

mit·denken, dachte mit, mitgedacht *to think along with*

erstklassig *first-class*
handgeschrieben *handwritten*
perfekt *perfect*

14.

AVANA, Photo-Film-Produktion GmbH
sucht

FOTOMODELLE

(auch Anfänger) zur Publikation für seriöse Werbung. Bitte rufen Sie uns an: München 089/493855, Montag-Freitag
10–18 Uhr

WORTSCHATZ

143

der Anfänger, - *beginner*
das Fotomodell, -e *model*
die Publikation, -en *publication*

die Werbung, -en *advertisement*

seriös *serious*

15.

Warum lächelt sie so?

Sie ist zufrieden, sie fühlt sich frei. Sie hat Abwechslung.
Möchten Sie so lächeln? Arbeiten Sie bei uns:

Internationales Handelshaus
im Stadtzentrum sucht
erfahrene

TELEFONISTIN

Fließend Englisch Bedingung, Französisch erwünscht,
auch Büronebenarbeiten. Wir zahlen bis zu DM 2000,-.
Zuschriften an Postfach A3849584.

WORTSCHATZ

die Abwechslung, -en   *variety*
die Bedingung, -en   *requirement*
der Handel   *commerce*
die Nebenarbeit, -en   *extra work, side duty*
das Stadtzentrum, -tren   *center city*
die Telefonistin, -nen   *telephone operator (female)*

sich fühlen   *to feel*
lächeln   *to smile*
zahlen   *to pay*

erwünscht   *desired*
zufrieden   *satisfied*

16.

Deutscher Haushalt in Südfrankreich sucht

FRÖHLICHES MÄDCHEN

kinderlieb (4 Kinder— 2, 7, 8, 10 Jahre) mit guten
Kochkenntnissen. Auch für Hilfe im Haushalt.

Beste Bezahlung, Freizeit, eigenes Zimmer mit
Bad, Radio und Fernsehapparat

WORTSCHATZ

144

das Bad, ⸚er   *bath*
der Fernsehapparat, -e   *TV set*
die Freizeit   *free time*
der Haushalt, -e   *household*
die Hilfe   *help*

die Kochkenntnisse (*pl.*)   *cooking knowledge*

fröhlich   *happy*
kinderlieb   *fond of children*

ZUM BESPRECHEN

1. Angebot Nr. 1: Warum muß man als Verkäufer(in) auf einem Flughafen englische Sprachkenntnisse haben?
2. Angebot Nr. 2: Sie sind Verkäufer(in) bei Bonanza. Wie überzeugen Sie einen Kunden oder eine Kundin, daß er oder sie Jeans kaufen sollte?
3. Angebot Nr. 3: Was muß man tun, bevor man Deutschlehrer(in) wird? Beschreiben Sie die Qualitäten einer guten Lehrerin oder eines guten Lehrers.
4. Angebot Nr. 4: Was erwartet Siemens von einem Programmierer oder einer Programmiererin?
5. Angebot Nr. 5: Welche Qualifikationen braucht man als Discjockey in einer Diskothek?
6. Angebot Nr. 6: Welche Pflichten hat man a) als Nachtportier b) als Hausmädchen c) als Frau für die Küche?
7. Angebot Nr. 7: Welche Kenntnisse braucht ein Taxifahrer oder eine Taxifahrerin in einer Großstadt?
8. Angebot Nr. 8: In diesem Stellenangebot steht nicht, was man für das Gehalt tun muß. Raten Sie, was es für eine Arbeit sein könnte.
9. Angebot Nr. 9: Sie möchten Automobil-Verkäufer werden. Wie überzeugen Sie einen Kunden, ein Auto (und besonders einen Mercedes!) zu kaufen?
10. Angebot Nr. 10: Wieso sind die Stellungen in diesem Stellenangebot besonders vorteilhaft?
11. Angebot Nr. 11: Was muß man als Automechaniker und Tankwart bei einer Selbstbedienungs-Tankstelle machen? Betrachten Sie sich auch das Bild auf Seite p. 146!
12. Angebot Nr. 12: Nennen Sie einige Aufgaben eines Hausmeisters.
13. Angebot Nr. 13: Warum sollte eine Sekretärin ihr Lichtbild und ihren handgeschriebenen Lebenslauf an die Firma schicken?
14. Angebot Nr. 14: Wie muß man aussehen, um Fotomodell zu werden?
15. Angebot Nr. 15: Warum muß eine Telefonistin in einem internationalen Handelshaus englisch und französisch sprechen? Welche anderen Sprachen sind außerdem noch wichtig? Warum?
16. Angebot Nr. 16: Das Mädchen, das diese Stelle annimmt, wird viel arbeiten müssen. Warum?

ZUR AUSFÜHRLICHEN DISKUSSION

1. Um welche Stellung würden Sie sich bewerben? Warum?
2. Wählen Sie für jedes Stellenangebot einen Partner in der Klasse und spielen Sie die Rollen von Personalchef und Bewerber. Stellen Sie so viele Fragen wie möglich!
3. Schreiben Sie ein Stellenangebot. Dann führen Sie mit jemandem in der Klasse für diese Stellung ein Einstellungsgespräch.
4. Beantworten Sie eines dieser Stellenangebote. Schreiben Sie einen Brief mit kurzem Lebenslauf (siehe Beispiel auf Seite 146) an die angegebene Adresse.

Lebenslauf eines Kaufmanns

NAME:	Hans Mayer
GEBOREN:	21. 2. 1950
GEBURTSORT:	Düsseldorf
STAATSANGEHÖRIGKEIT:	deutsch
ELTERN:	Wilhelm Mayer, Omnibusfahrer
	Hedwig Mayer (geborene Brandhoff), Verkäuferin
FAMILIENSTAND:	ledig
SCHULBILDUNG:	8 Jahre Volksschule
	2 Jahre Berufsschule. Kaufmännischer Zweig
WEHRDIENST:	18 Monate
BERUFSTÄTIGKEIT:	2½ Jahre Großhandelskaufmann, Verkäufer, Einkäufer
	1 Jahr Abteilungsleiter

Ein Automechaniker

1. Was macht der Automechaniker?
2. Was bedeutet: „Wir prüfen und erneuern zu günstigen Preisen".

Eine deutsche Sekretärin in Frankfurt

1. Was macht die Sekretärin?
2. Beschreiben Sie die Dinge auf ihrem Schreibtisch.
3. Nennen Sie einige Pflichten einer guten Sekretärin.

IHR IDEALPARTNER 15

A. Heiratsanzeigen/Bekanntschaften

☎ 089/2377-777

Männlich

1.

Junger Mann, Karl, sucht Mädchen (18-28 Jahre) mit braunen Augen und Sommersprossen, liebenswert, häuslich, für gemeinsame Wochenenden. Ich bin 30/178* Junggeselle, sehbehindert. Mädchen darf mollig sein. Führerschein erwünscht. Zuschriften an Postfach 1158.

WORTSCHATZ

das Auge, -n *eye*
der Führerschein, -e *driver's license*
der Junggeselle, -n *bachelor*
das Postfach, ⁼er *P.O. box*
die Sommersprossen (*pl.*) *freckles*
das Wochenende, -n *weekend*

gemeinsam *mutual, together*
häuslich *domestic*
liebenswert *dear, worthy of love*
mollig *pleasingly plump*
sehbehindert *visually impaired*

2.

Werner, 32 jähriger Schiffsoffizier, zur Zeit in Haft, 178, schlank, sportlich, wünscht Freundschaft mit toleranter, junger Dame bis 30. Postfach 8043.

WORTSCHATZ

die Freundschaft, -en *friendship*
die Haft *arrest, imprisonment*
der Schiffsoffizier, -e *ship's officer*

wünschen *to wish*

schlank *slender, slim*
sportlich *athletic*
tolerant *tolerant*

zur Zeit *at this time, presently*

149

---

*30/178 = 30 Jahre alt/178 cm. groß
(170 cm. = 5′ 7″; 175 cm. = 5′ 9″; 180 cm. = 5′ 11″, 185 cm. = 6′ 1″)

3.

Erfahrener Mann, Rechtsanwalt in den besten Jahren, hat wochentags viel Zeit und will Unterhaltung, Diskussion usw. Welches Mädchen, welche Dame, telefoniert so gerne wie ich? Ihr Gesprächsstoff kann unproblematisch, problematisch und sogar absurd sein. Auf jede Zuschrift erfolgt mein Telefonanruf. Zuschriften an Postfach 9268.

WORTSCHATZ

die Diskussion, -en   *discussion*
der Gesprächsstoff, -e   *conversational material*
der Rechtsanwalt, ⁼e   *lawyer*
der Telefonanruf, -e   *telephone call*
die Unterhaltung, -en   *conversation, entertainment*

erfolgen auf (+ acc.)   *to follow*
telefonieren   *to telephone*

problematisch   *problematic*
wochentags   *weekdays*

so . . . wie   *as . . . as*

4.

Ich heiße Peter, bin Witwer, Rentner, 77 Jahre, 1,68 m, jugendliche Figur, rüstig, temperamentvoll, gepflegtes Aussehen, zur Zeit mit Gipsbein. Suche nettes, wohlproportioniertes Mädchen bis 25 Jahre, das jeden Dienstag um die Mittagszeit mit mir ins Schwimmbad geht. Auch zum Liebhaben und Schmusen.

WORTSCHATZ

das Aussehen   *appearance*
die Figur, -en   *figure*
das Gipsbein, -e   *plaster cast on leg*
das Liebhaben   *fondness, love*
die Mittagszeit, -en   *noon time*
der Rentner, -   *pensioner*
das Schmusen   *kissing, "necking"*
das Schwimmbad, ⁼er   *swimming pool*

der Witwer, -   *widower*

gepflegt   *well-groomed*
jugendlich   *youthful*
nett   *nice*
rüstig   *hale and hearty*
temperamentvoll   *lively*
wohlproportioniert   *well-proportioned*

5.

Fisch, 31/172, schlank, blaue Augen, Nichtraucher, erfolgreicher Architekt mit viel Zeit, offen, nett, herzlich, romantisch, unkompliziert, treu, sportlich—Tennis, Reiten, Skifahren, Segeln, Rallyesport, Sportwagen (Mercedes 450 SLC), Segeljacht am Chiemsee,* reiselustig, viel Urlaub, seit 1 Woche geschieden (schuldlos). Suche junges, hübsches, liebes, herzliches, nicht-rauchendes Mädchen, welches sich gerne verwöhnen läßt und mit mir die Freizeit genießen will. Für jede Zuschrift mit Foto gibt's ein Rendezvous, unter Postfach 1158.

WORTSCHATZ

der Fisch, -e *Pisces (astrology), fish*
das Foto, -s *photograph*
die Freizeit *free time*
der Nichtraucher, - *non-smoker*
der Rallyesport *rally sports*
das Reiten *horseback riding*
das Rendezvous, - *rendezvous*
die Segeljacht, -en *sailing yacht*
das Segeln *sailing*
das Skifahren *skiing*
der Sportwagen, - *sports car*
der Urlaub, -e *vacation*

verwöhnen *to spoil*

erfolgreich *successful*
geschieden *divorced*
herzlich *affectionate, warm*
hübsch *pretty, cute*
lieb *dear*
nicht-rauchend *non-smoking*
reiselustig *fond of travelling*
romantisch *romantic*
schuldlos *guiltless(ly)*
treu *faithful*

genießen, genoß, genossen *to enjoy*

* Ein See in Bayern

6.

> Düsseldorferin, 25/170, blond, schlank, grüne Augen, sportlich, wünscht Freundschaft mit nettem, aufgeschlossenem Partner für Freizeit und Urlaub. Bildzuschrift an Postfach 4098.

WORTSCHATZ _____

die Bildzuschrift, -en *letter with photo*
die Düsseldorferin, -nen *woman from Düsseldorf*
der Partner, - *partner (male)*

die Partnerin, -nen *partner (female)*

aufgeschlossen *open, accessible*

7

> Apartes Sunny-girl, Mannequintyp, 25/160, mit Niveau, voller Charme und Esprit, sucht reiferen, großzügigen Gentleman für interessante Freizeit. Zuschriften an Postfach 6907.

WORTSCHATZ _____

152

der Charme *charm*
der Esprit *esprit*
das Niveau *class*
der Typ, -en *type*

apart *attractive, special*
großzügig *generous*
reif *mature*

8.

In 24 Stunden nicht mehr allein! So ein Tag, so wunderschön wie heute . . . der dürfte nie vergehen. Ach, in
der Wohnstube, da sitzen wir . . . vor uns eine Flasche
Bier . . . und träumen von einer schönen Verlobungsfeier. GISELA, bildhübsch, 19/167, knipst die Stehlampe
aus . . . denn schöner klingt's im Dämmerlicht, was ich
Dir leise sage: ,,Ich liebe Dich." Doch vergeht der Tag
ohne Verlobungsring—wenn Du erfährst, daß ich in
bittrer Armut lebe? Schreib schnell Deine Antwort mit
Foto unter Nr. 2140.

WORTSCHATZ

die Armut *poverty*
das Dämmerlicht *twilight*
die Stehlampe, -n *floor lamp*
die Verlobungsfeier, -n *engagement
  celebration*
der Verlobungsring, -e *engagement
  ring*
die Wohnstube, -n *family room*

aus·knipsen *to turn off*

erfahren (erfährt), erfuhr, erfahren *to
  learn, find out*
klingen *to sound*
träumen *to dream*
vergehen, verging, ist vergangen *to
  pass away, perish*

bildhübsch *extremely pretty*
bitter *bitter*
wunderschön *gorgeous, beautiful*

9.

Suchst Du eine Bäuerin für Deinen Hof? Ich bin die
ideale Frau für Dich: Anne, 20 Jahre, ledig und hübsch,
stark, liebt Tiere und Landwirtschaft. Zuschriften an Postfach 5841.

WORTSCHATZ

der Bauer, -n *farmer (male)*
die Bäuerin, -nen *farmer (female)*
der Hof, ⁼e *farm*
die Landwirtschaft *argriculture*
das Tier, -e *animal*

sich eignen zu *to be suited, qualified
  for*

ideal *ideal*
ledig *single*
stark *strong*

153

10.

> Rufen Sie mich an. Angelika, 20, brünett, häuslich, möchte gerne verständnisvollen Lebenspartner, der sich für Wandern, Autofahren, Fernsehen, Sport und Biergartengespräche interessiert. Ich bin Arbeiterin, hübsch, sympathisch, ehrlich, treu und herzensgut. Ich habe eine gemütliche Wohnung sowie Ersparnisse. Schreiben Sie an Postfach 5171. Antwort mit Foto kommt sofort!

WORTSCHATZ

die Arbeiterin, -nen *worker (female)*
das Autofahren *driving*
die Ersparnisse (*pl.*) *savings*
das Gespräch, -e *conversation*
der Sport, -arten *sports*
das Wandern *hiking*

sich interessieren für *to have an interest in*

brünett *brunette*
ehrlich *honest*
gemütlich *comfortable*
herzensgut *kind-hearted*
sympathisch *congenial, likeable*
verständnisvoll *understanding*

ZUM BESPRECHEN

1. Anzeige Nr. 1: Warum braucht der junge Mann ein Mädchen mit Führerschein?
2. Anzeige Nr. 2: Warum möchte der Schiffsoffizier eine tolerante Dame finden?
3. Anzeige Nr. 3: Der erfahrene Rechtsanwalt ist „in den besten Jahren". Welches sind Ihrer Meinung nach die „besten" Jahre? Warum? Wie alt könnte der Mann sein?
4. Anzeige Nr. 4: Der Witwer Peter ist alt aber temperamentvoll. Wie ist er zu seinem Gipsbein gekommen? Warum sucht er ein so junges Mädchen?
5. Anzeige Nr. 5: Der schlanke „Fisch" mit dem Mercedes will sein Mädchen verwöhnen. Wie kann man ein Mädchen verwöhnen? Machen Sie eine Liste!
6. Anzeige Nr. 6: Eine Dame aus Düsseldorf ist eine Düsseldorferin. Wie heißt ein Mädchen aus Hamburg? Aus Berlin? Aus Wien? Aus New York?
7. Anzeige Nr. 7: Das aparte Sunny-girl sucht einen großzügigen Gentleman. Was werden die beiden in ihrer Freizeit wahrscheinlich zusammen machen?
8. Anzeige Nr. 8: Gisela ist sehr romantisch, aber arm. Glauben Sie, daß Liebe wichtiger ist als Geld? Warum? Warum nicht?
9. Anzeige Nr. 9: Weshalb eignet sich Anne sicher gut zum Beruf der Bäuerin? Begründen Sie Ihre Antwort.
10. Anzeige Nr. 10: Die brünette Angelika interessiert sich für Biergartengespräche. Wieso ist ein Biergartengespräch besonders gemütlich?

ZUR AUSFÜHRLICHEN DISKUSSION

1. Sie sind intelligent, jung, schön, aber einsam. Welche Partnerin oder welchen Partner würden Sie wählen? Warum?

2. Sie interessieren sich für einen Mann/ein Mädchen in den Heiratsanzeigen. Der Mann/ das Mädchen sitzt neben Ihnen in der Klasse! Wählen Sie eine Anzeige aus und befragen Sie persönlich Ihren zukünftigen Partner oder Ihre zukünftige Partnerin.

3. Schreiben Sie Ihre eigene Heiratsanzeige. Lesen Sie sie der Klasse vor. Möchte jemand in der Klasse *Sie* als Partner haben? Warum? Warum nicht?

4. Gibt es auch Heiratsanzeigen in den Zeitungen und Zeitschriften Amerikas? Glauben Sie, daß Heiratsanzeigen nützlich sind? Nennen Sie einige Vorteile und Nachteile solcher Anzeigen.

5. Würden *Sie* jemanden durch eine Heiratsanzeige suchen, wenn Sie einsam wären? Begründen Sie Ihre Antwort.

B. Partner-Test

MACHEN SIE DIESEN GRATIS-TEST:
SIE ERFAHREN, WELCHE HEIRATS-CHANCEN SIE HABEN.
DAZU ERHALTEN SIE KOSTENLOS DIE BESCHREIBUNG
IHRES IDEALPARTNERS,
DEN DER COMPUTER FÜR SIE GEFUNDEN HAT!

1
Interessen-Diagramm

Kreuzen Sie an, was Sie in ihrer Freizeit bevorzugen. Denn ihr Idealpartner soll in seinen Interessen zu Ihnen passen

sehr inter-essiert	gele-gent-lich	kein Inter-esse	
☐	☐	☐	aktiv Sport treiben
☐	☐	☐	Besuch von Sportveranstaltungen
☐	☐	☐	Funk and Fernsehen Unterhaltungssendungen
☐	☐	☐	Sendungen über Politik und Wissenschaft
☐	☐	☐	Krimis
☐	☐	☐	Musiksendungen
☐	☐	☐	Naturwissenschaft/ Technik
☐	☐	☐	Problemfilme
☐	☐	☐	Sportsendungen
☐	☐	☐	Geisteswissenschaften
☐	☐	☐	Basteln/Handarbeiten
☐	☐	☐	Musizieren
☐	☐	☐	ernste Musik hören
☐	☐	☐	Unterhaltungsmusik
☐	☐	☐	Bildungslektüre
☐	☐	☐	Unterhaltungslektüre
☐	☐	☐	Theater, Oper, Konzert
☐	☐	☐	Tanzen
☐	☐	☐	Parties
☐	☐	☐	Diskussionen
☐	☐	☐	Wandern, Bergsteigen
☐	☐	☐	mit Auto spazierenfahren
☐	☐	☐	Urlaub Körperl. Betätigung u. Sport
☐	☐	☐	Faulenzen
☐	☐	☐	Bildung
☐	☐	☐	Vergnügungen
☐	☐	☐	Familienfeiern

2
Psychologischer Farbtest

In das Feld der Farbe, die Ihnen am besten gefällt, schreiben Sie eine 1. Die Farbe, die Ihnen am zweitbesten gefällt, bekommt eine 2.

dunkelblau	leuchtend gelb	
mittelgrau	feuerrot	grasgrün

⤵ 3 ↙
PARTNER-PROFIL

Erscheinung

☐ sportlich	☐ repräsentativ
☐ modisch	☐ solide
☐ elegant	☐ salopp

Figur

☐ schlank	☐ stattlich
☐ mittelschlank	☐ korpulent
☐ kräftig	

Eigenschaften

Wählen Sie aus den folgenden Eigenschaften 5 aus, die Sie von Ihrer zukünftigen Partnerin erwarten:

☐ temperament-voll	☐ strebsam
☐ fröhlich	☐ natürlich
☐ intelligent	☐ gütig
☐ ehrlich	☐ sportlich
☐ sparsam	☐ gutaussehend
☐ häuslich	☐ selbsbewuBt

5
BILDUNG

Beschreiben Sie Ihre
Schulbildung: _____
_____
_____

Schule: _____

Zukünftiger Beruf: _____

Monatliches Einkommen:
☐ bis zu 600.—DM
☐ bis zu 1500.—DM
☐ bis zu 3000.—DM
☐ über 3000.—DM

6
Ehe und Religion

☐ Sind Sie ledig	☐ konfessionslos
☐ verwitwet	☐ evangelisch
☐ geschieden	☐ katholisch
	☐ jüdisch
	andere_____

4
Biologische und soziologische Daten

Wie lautet Ihre genaue Anschrift? ☐ Herr ☐ Frau ☐ Fräulein

Vorname: _____ wohnhaft bei:_____

Name: _____ Telefon: _____

StraBe: _____ Ihre Staatsangehörigkeit: _____

PLZ/Wohnort: _____ Geburtsdatum: _____

KörpergröBe_____cm_____

die Anschrift, -en *address*
das Bergsteigen *mountain climbing*
der Beruf, -e *profession, occupation*
die Betätigung, -en *activity*
die Bildung *education*
die Bildungslektüre *educational literature*
das Datum, -ten *date*
das Einkommen, - *income*
die Eigenschaft, -en *quality*
die Erscheinung, -en *appearance*
die Familienfeier, -n *family celebration*
das Feld, -er *field, square*
die Figur, -en *figure*
das Formular, -e *form*
die Geisteswissenschaften *humanities*
die Handarbeit, -en *needlework*
das Interesse, -n *interest*
die Körpergröße, -n *height*
der Krimi, -s *detective story*
die Musiksendung, -en *musical program*
die Naturwissenschaft, -en *natural science*
die Oper, -n *opera*
der Opernbesuch, -e *opera attendance*
die Party, -ies *party*
die Politik *politics*
der Problemfilm, -e *movie with artistic merit*
die Sportveranstaltung, -en *sports event*
die Staatsangehörigkeit, -en *citizenship*
die Technik *technical science*
der Test, -s *test*
das Theater, - *theater*
der Theaterbesuch, -e *theater attendance*
die Unterhaltungslektüre, -n *popular literature*
die Unterhaltungsmusik *popular music*
die Unterhaltungssendung, -en *entertainment program*
die Vergnügung, -en *pleasure*
der Vorname, -ns, -n *first name*
die Wissenschaft, -en *science*

an·kreuzen *to check*
aus·füllen *to fill out*
basteln *to work with metal, paper, or wood as a hobby*
bevorzugen *to prefer*
faulenzen *to be idle, laze around*
feiern *to celebrate*
gefallen (gefällt), gefiel, gefallen (+ dat.) *to please*
musizieren *to play music*
tanzen *to dance*
wandern *to hike*

evangelisch *Protestant*
fröhlich *happy, cheerful*
gelegentlich *occasionally*
geschieden *divorced*
gutaussehend *good-looking*
gütig *kind, benevolent*
jüdisch *Jewish*
katholisch *Catholic*
konfessionslos *without religious affiliation*
körperlich *physical*
korpulent *corpulent, fat*
kräftig *strong*
modisch *fashionable*
monatlich *monthly*
repräsentativ *distinguished*
salopp *relaxed, informal*
selbstbewußt *self-confident*
solide *reliable*
sparsam *thrifty*
stattlich *portly*
strebsam *ambitious, industrious*
verwitwet *widowed*

mit dem Auto spazieren fahren (fährt spazieren), fuhr spazieren, ist spazieren gefahren *to drive around*
passen zu *to fit, be suitable for*
Sport treiben, trieb, getrieben *to play sports*
wohnhaft bei *care of (c/o)*

ZUM BESPRECHEN

1. Welche Interessen sind Ihrer Meinung nach am wichtigsten? Begründen Sie Ihre Antwort!
2. Psychologischer Farbtest. Interpretieren Sie *selber* die Psyche von Menschen, die die folgenden Farben bevorzugen: a) gelb b) grau c) feuerrot d) grasgrün.
3. Partner-Profil: Wählen Sie die besten Eigenschaften einer Person aus und verteidigen Sie Ihre Wahl.
4. Füllen Sie Formular Nr. 4 („Biologische und soziologische Daten") aus.
   a) Sollte Ihr Partner oder Ihre Partnerin aus demselben Wohnort kommen?
   b) Sollte Ihr Partner oder Ihre Partnerin älter oder jünger sein als Sie? Warum?
   c) Wie groß sollte er oder sie sein (160 cm. = 5′ 3″; 165 cm. = 5′ 5″; 170 cm. = 5′ 7″; 175 cm. = 5′ 9″ usw.)?
   d) Wie schwer sollte er oder sie sein (1 kg. = 2.2 lbs., 45,4 kg. = 100 lbs.; 58, 7 kg. = 130 lbs.; 72,4 kg. = 160 lbs.; 86,0 kg. = 190 lbs.)?
5. Beschreiben Sie Ihre Schulbildung. Welche Bildung sollte Ihr Partner oder Ihre Partnerin haben? Wieviel Geld sollte er oder sie verdienen?
6. Welchen Beruf sollte Ihr Partner oder Ihre Partnerin haben?
7. Muß der Partner/die Partnerin dieselbe Religion wie Sie haben?
8. Füllen Sie das Formular aus. Schreiben Sie dann Ihr eigenes psychologisches Persönlichkeitsprofil und Ihr Partnerprofil.
9. Sollte Ihr Partner oder Ihre Partnerin Ihre Interessen teilen? Oder wollen Sie jemanden, der andere Interessen hat als Sie? Warum?
10. Unterhalten Sie sich mit einem Klassenkameraden, der das Formular ausgefüllt hat. Stellen Sie an ihn oder sie Fragen über die Details, die Sie am interessantesten finden. Spielen Sie die Rolle eines Psychologen.
11. Beschreiben Sie Menschen, die a) häuslich b) strebsam c) gütig sind.

ZUR AUSFÜHRLICHEN DISKUSSION

1. Mein Idealpartner/meine Idealpartnerin. Beschreiben Sie ihn/sie.
2. Sollte der Partner (die Partnerin) auch der Idealpartner (die Idealpartnerin) sein? Erläutern Sie Ihre Antwort.
3. Psychologische Tests sind bedeutungslos und dumm. Was halten Sie von dieser Ansicht?
4. Man braucht einen Computer, um den Idealpartner (die Idealpartnerin) zu finden. Welches Argument spricht a) dafür b) dagegen?

FRAGEN SIE
DR. PAUL MÜLLER
16

HABEN SIE PROBLEME IN DER LIEBE, SCHULE ODER
FAMILIE?
DANN SCHREIBEN SIE AN DR. MÜLLER.
ER ANTWORTET IN *DEUTSCHE REVUE* ODER VER-
TRAULICH IM BRIEF.

An Dr. Paul Müller
DEUTSCHE REVUE
Rheinstr. 15

8000 München 40

1. Betrogen und enttäuscht

Die Männer suchen ihren Spaß—
ich will Liebe.

Lieber Herr Dr. Müller!

Mein Freund hat mich belogen und betrogen. Dann lernte ich einen anderen Mann kennen, dem ich vertraute, bis ich erkannte, daß auch er mich schamlos belog. Jetzt fühle ich mich einsam und leer. Ich suche Wärme, Liebe und Verständnis—die Männer suchen nur ihren Spaß. Männer mit Herz gibt es heute nicht mehr. Haben Sie einen guten Rat für mich?

schreibt Renate K. (18)

WORTSCHATZ

der Berater, - *adviser*
der Freund, -e *friend, boyfriend*
der Herzenskummer *sadness of the heart*
die Liebe *love*
der Ratschlag, ⁻e *piece of advice, suggestion*
der Spaß, ⁻e *fun, amusement*
das Verständnis *understanding*
die Wärme *warmth*

belügen, belog, belogen *to lie to (someone)*
betrügen, betrog, betrogen *to deceive (someone)*

sich fühlen *to feel*
kennen·lernen *to become acquainted (with)*
lösen *to solve*
vertrauen (+ dat.) *to trust*
vor·lesen (liest vor), las vor, vorgelesen *to present, to read aloud*

betrogen *deceived*
einsam *lonesome, lonely*
enttäuscht *disappointed*
leer *empty*
schamlos *shameless(ly)*

einen guten Rat geben *to give a good piece of advice*

ZUM BESPRECHEN

1. Renate schreibt nicht, wie die zwei Männer sie belogen und betrogen haben. Was könnten die Männer gemacht haben?
2. Stimmt es, daß „Männer nur ihren Spaß suchen"? Erläutern Sie Ihre Antwort.
3. Haben Sie einen guten Rat für die arme Renate? Schreiben Sie ihr eine Antwort. Lesen Sie dann die Antwort Dr. Müllers auf Seite 164!
4. Schreiben Sie selbst einen Brief an Dr. Müller über einen schweren Herzenskummer. Lesen Sie ihn der Klasse vor. Ihre Klassenkameraden übernehmen dann spontan die Rolle Dr. Müllers.

161

2. Berechtigt oder unberechtigt?

Muß man den Hausschlüssel beim Hauswirt lassen?

Lieber Herr Dr. Müller!

Ich will mit meiner Frau und meiner Tochter in die Ferien fahren. Da wir seit kurzem in einer neuen Wohnung wohnen, will der Hauswirt während unserer Abwesenheit den Wohnungsschlüssel haben. Was kann ich dagegen tun? Muß ich ihm den Schlüssel geben?

schreibt Hermann B. (32)

WORTSCHATZ

die Abwesenheit *absence*
der Hauswirt, -e *landlord*
der Schlüssel, - *key*
die Wohnung, -en *apartment*

sorgen für *to take care of*

berechtigt *justified*
unberechtigt *unjustified*

in die Ferien fahren *to take a vacation*
seit kurzem *since recently*

ZUM BESPRECHEN

1. Welche Vor- und Nachteile hat es für Sie, Ihren Hausschlüssel bei einem Freund oder einer Freundin zu lassen?
2. Haben Sie einen guten Rat für Herrn B.? Schreiben Sie ihn auf, und lesen Sie dann die Antwort Dr. Müllers auf Seite 164.
3. Sie machen eine Reise, die einen Monat dauert. Sie bitten Ihren Freund oder Ihre Freundin, für Ihre Wohnung zu sorgen. Sagen Sie ihm/ihr alles, was er/sie während Ihrer Abwesenheit machen muß. Natürlich hat er/sie Fragen an Sie.

3. In den Lehrer verknallt

Ich habe mich in meinen Lehrer verliebt,
und mein Freund weiß Bescheid.

Lieber Herr Dr. Müller!

Ich bin dieses Schuljahr in eine neue Schule gekommen, weil wir umgezogen sind. Unser Klassenlehrer ist fünfundzwanzig Jahre alt und sieht sehr gut aus. Ich kann mir nicht helfen—ich habe mich auf den ersten Blick in ihn verknallt. Da mein Freund in meiner Klasse ist, weiß er davon und will mit mir Schluß machen. Wenn mein Lehrer mich etwas fragt, kann ich kein Wort sagen. Ich starre ihn immer nur an. Helfen Sie mir, Herr Dr. Müller, denn ich möchte meinen Freund auf keinen Fall verlieren.

schreibt Nora W. (13)

WORTSCHATZ

der Blick, -e *look, glance*
der Lehrer, - *teacher (male)*
die Lehrerin, -nen *teacher (female)*

an·starren *to stare at*
sich benehmen (benimmt sich), benahm sich, sich benommen *to behave*
drohen (+ dat.) *to threaten*
um·ziehen, zog um, ist umgezogen *to move (domicile)*

auf keinen Fall *in no case*
Bescheid wissen *to know what's going on*
Schluß machen *to terminate*
sich in jemanden verlieben (oder verknallen) *to fall in love with someone*

ZUM BESPRECHEN

1. Glauben Sie, daß Nora zu jung ist, um in ihren Lehrer verliebt zu sein? Warum?
2. Spielen Sie die Rolle des Dr. Müller. Was soll die kleine Nora tun? Lesen Sie dann die Antwort auf Seite 165.
3. Wie benimmt sich ein Mädchen, wenn es sich in jemanden verliebt?
4. Wie benimmt sich ein Junge, wenn er sich in jemanden verliebt?

Herr Dr. Müller Antwortet

1. Herr Dr. Müller antwortet Renate K. (Betrogen und enttäuscht)

Liebe Renate!

Sie haben in Ihrem Leben schon zwei Enttäuschungen erlebt und sind verbittert. Deshalb Ihr hartes Urteil über „die Männer". Es ist ungerecht, glauben Sie mir, und viele Briefe, die ich erhalte, beweisen es. Männer mit Herz und menschlicher Wärme gibt es allemal, nur müssen Sie Geduld haben.

WORTSCHATZ

die Enttäuschung, -en *disappointment*
die Geduld *patience*
das Urteil, -e *judgment, decision*

beweisen, bewies, bewiesen *to prove*
erhalten (erhält), erhielt, erhalten *to receive*
erleben *to experience*

glauben (+ dat. with people) *to believe*

allemal *always*
menschlich *human*
ungerecht *unfair*
verbittert *bitter*

2. Herr Dr. Müller antwortet Hermann B. (Berechtigt oder unberechtigt?)

Der Hauswirt muß die Möglichkeit haben, in dringenden Fällen in die Wohnung zu gelangen. Damit der Hauswirt das wirklich nur in dringenden Fällen macht, versiegeln Sie den Schlüssel in einem Briefumschlag. Falls der Umschlag nach Ihrer Rückkehr geöffnet ist, muß Ihnen der Hauswirt den Grund erklären.

WORTSCHATZ

der Briefumschlag, ⸚e *envelope*
der Fall, ⸚e *case, event*
der Grund, ⸚e *reason*
die Rückkehr *return*

gelangen *to get admitted to, to reach*

versiegeln *to seal*

dringend *urgent*
falls *in case*
geöffnet *open*

164

3. Herr Dr. Müller antwortet Nora W. (In den Lehrer verknallt)

Zu Deinem Brief gibt es einiges zu sagen. Erstens: Du kannst Dich verlieben, in wen Du willst. Jeder Mensch hat das freie Recht, sich zu verlieben, wann, wie, wo und wie oft er will. Soweit ist das nämlich eine Privatsache. Zweitens: Du bist minderjährig. Vielleicht mag der Lehrer Dich auch gern, aber es wäre für ihn eine Katastrophe, der Ruin seiner Existenz, vielleicht sogar seines Lebens, wenn er Deine Gefühle erwidern würde. Man würde ihn als Lehrer feuern, und vielleicht käme er sogar ins Gefängnis. Ich kann mir nicht vorstellen, daß Du gerade den Mann, in den Du verliebt bist, in Gefahr bringen willst. Drittens: Man soll andere Menschen nicht in Versuchung führen, denn dann wird man selber schuldig. Viertens: Es geht nicht um Deinen Freund und was er will. Fünftens: Du mußt lernen, daß im Leben nicht alles so geht, wie man will.

WORTSCHATZ

das Gefängnis, -se	*jail*	drittens	*thirdly*
das Gefühl, -e	*feeling*	erstens	*first*
die Privatsache, -n	*matter of privacy*	fünftens	*fifthly*
das Recht, -e	*right, privilege*	minderjährig	*juvenile, under age*
		schuldig	*guilty*
erwidern	*to reply, return, reciprocate*	viertens	*fourthly*
feuern	*to fire*	zweitens	*secondly*
gehen um	*to have to do with*		
sich vor·stellen	*to imagine*		

ZUM BESPRECHEN

1. Stimmen Sie mit den Antworten Dr. Müllers überein? Oder glauben Sie, daß er zu konservativ ist? Wie unterscheiden sich Ihre Antworten von seinen in den einzelnen Fällen?
2. Gibt es auch in Amerika einen Dr. Müller? Lesen Sie solche Briefe in der Zeitung gern? Warum oder warum nicht?
3. Warum schreibt Dr. Müller „Du" im dritten Brief, aber „Sie" in den ersten beiden Briefen?
4. Kann Ihnen ein Ratgeber überhaupt helfen, wenn Sie ein Problem haben? Wenn ja, warum? Wenn nein, warum nicht?

165

HOROSKOP: IHRE STERNE

17

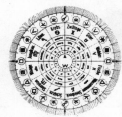 **Ihre Sterne**

 WIDDER 21. 3. bis 20. 4.:
Ein Mensch, der erst kürzlich in Ihr Leben getreten ist, wird Ihnen bald unentbehrlich sein. Bei einem Wettbewerb können Sie eine Menge Geld gewinnen.

 STIER 21. 4. bis 20. 5.:
Gäste, mit denen Sie nicht gerechnet hatten, melden sich an. Sie sollten Ihnen willkommen sein, auch wenn das einige Unbequemlichkeiten mit sich bringt.

 ZWILLINGE 21. 5. bis 21. 6.:
In der Liebe werden Sie jetzt unzufrieden werden. Eigentlich sollten Sie in diesem Monat nichts Neues mehr anfangen. Es brächte Sie nur in Bedrängnis, denn Sie haben bereits erreicht, was möglich ist.

 KREBS 22. 6. bis 22. 7.:
Sie haben viel gelernt, aber anscheinend reizt es Sie mehr, sich mit Dingen zu befassen, die neu für Sie sind. Dabei ist jedoch einige Vorsicht geboten.

 LÖWE 23. 7. bis 23. 8.:
Kleine Auseinandersetzungen sind nicht tragisch. Aber Vorsicht! Tun Sie etwas mehr für Ihre Gesundheit—wie oft muß man Ihnen das noch sagen?

166

 JUNGFRAU 24. 8. bis 23. 9.:
Neue Partner, mit denen Sie zu tun haben, kalkulieren sehr genau. Fragen Sie nicht andere in Dingen um Rat, die nur Sie allein entscheiden können.

WAAGE 24. 9. bis 23. 10.:
Seien Sie ein wenig wählerischer. Bestimmt verlieren Sie nichts, wenn Sie das eine oder andere Angebot ablehnen. Am Wochenende viel Sonne in der Liebe.

SKORPION 24. 10. bis 22. 11.:
Sie müssen wissen, was Sie wollen, und es den anderen dann auch klar sagen. Sonst nehmen die Auseinandersetzungen und Reibereien kein Ende mehr.

SCHÜTZE 23. 11. bis 21. 12.:
Sparsamkeit kann zu weit gehen. Wenn Sie Ihr Geld einigermaßen geschickt verwenden, können Sie mehr davon haben. Allerdings gehört etwas Planung dazu.

STEINBOCK 22. 12. bis 21. 1.:
Sie vermissen manches. Vergessen Sie darüber aber nicht ganz, was Sie haben. Das ist nicht wenig. Eine Beziehung könnte vertieft werden. Die Unterzeichnung eines Vertrages sollte bald abgeschlossen sein.

WASSERMANN 22. 1. bis 20. 2.:
Geselligkeit, Flirt, Geschenke und nette Briefe—alle kleinen Freuden des Lebens werden Sie bald genießen. Das Ergebnis einer Prüfung übertrifft Ihre Erwartungen. Nützen Sie die Gunst der Stunde, anstatt erst eine Pause einzulegen.

FISCHE 21. 2. bis 20. 3.:
Nehmen Sie neue Kontakte auf. Für das, was Sie planen, kann man gar nicht genug Beziehungen haben. Hoffentlich schätzen Sie Ihre Möglichkeiten und Chancen richtig ein.

WORTSCHATZ

das Angebot, -e *offer*
die Auseinandersetzung, -en *argument*
die Bedrängnis, -se *trouble, distress*
die Beziehung, -en *relationship*
das Ergebnis, -se *result*
die Erwartung, -en *expectancy*
der Flirt, -s *flirtation*
die Geselligkeit *social life*
die Gesundheit *health*
die Gunst *favor, good will*
das Horoskop, -e *horoscope*
der Kontakt, -e *contact*
die Pause, -n *pause*
die Planung *planning*
der Rat (*pl.* die Ratschläge) *advice*
die Reiberei, -en *conflict*

die Sparsamkeit *thriftiness*
das Sternzeichen, - *sign (astrology)*
die Unbequemlichkeit, -en *discomfort*
die Unterzeichnung, -en *signature*
der Vertrag, ⁻e *contract*
die Vorsicht *precaution, care*
der Wettbewerb, -e *contest*

ab·lehnen *to refuse*
ab·schließen, schloß ab, abgeschlossen *to conclude*
sich an·melden *to announce oneself*
sich befassen (mit) *to occupy oneself (with)*
sich entscheiden, entschied sich, sich entschieden *to decide*

167

erreichen *to reach*
gehören (zu) *to belong (to)*
genießen, genoß, genossen *to enjoy*
gewinnen, gewann, gewonnen *to win*
kalkulieren *to calculate*
rechnen *to figure*
reizen *to excite, stimulate*
vermissen *to miss*
verwenden *to use*

allerdings *of course*
anscheinend *apparently*
bereits *already*
eigentlich *real(ly)*

einigermaßen *to some extent*
geschickt *skillful, adroit*

eine Menge Geld *a heap of money*
erst kürzlich *just a short time ago*
jemandem das Horoskop stellen *to read someone's horoscope*
kein Ende nehmen *to have no end*
Kontakte an·knüpfen *to make contacts*
in Bedrängnis bringen *to get in trouble*
um Rat fragen *to ask for advice*
Vorsicht! *Be careful!*

ZUM BESPRECHEN

1. Wann sind Sie geboren?
2. Was ist Ihr Sternzeichen?
3. Lesen Sie Ihr Horoskop und übersetzen Sie es!
4. WIDDER: Was machen Sie mit dem Geld, das Sie gewinnen werden?
5. STIER: Was tun Sie, wenn unangemeldete Gäste vor Ihrer Tür stehen?
6. ZWILLINGE: Nennen Sie einiges, was Sie bereits in diesem Monat erreicht haben.
7. KREBS: Sie befassen sich gerne mit Dingen, die neu für Sie sind. Was haben Sie im letzten Jahr Neues gemacht?
8. LÖWE: Nennen Sie einige Dinge, die Sie für Ihre Gesundheit tun können.
9. JUNGFRAU: Treffen Sie Ihre eigenen Entscheidungen, oder müssen Sie andere Menschen um Rat fragen? Warum?
10. WAAGE: Viel Sonne in der Liebe fürs Wochende! Was planen Sie für dieses Wochenende?
11. SKORPION: Sie wissen genau, was Sie wollen. Welche Ziele möchten Sie im nächsten Jahr erreichen?
12. SCHÜTZE: Sie sind ein sparsamer Mensch, aber wie werden Sie Ihr Geld im nächsten Jahr geschickt verwenden?
13. STEINBOCK: Obwohl Sie manches vermissen, haben Sie trotzdem viel. Seien Sie positiv! Beschreiben Sie das Wichtigste, das Sie schon haben.
14. WASSERMANN: Das Ergebnis einer Prüfung übertrifft Ihre Erwartungen. Beschreiben Sie einige wichtige Prüfungen, die Sie im nächsten Monat machen werden.
15. FISCHE: Man kann nie genug Beziehungen haben. Nennen Sie einige neue Kontakte, die Sie im letzten Monat angeknüpft haben.

ZUR AUSFÜHRLICHEN DISKUSSION

1. Stellen Sie einem Klassenkameraden das Horoskop:
   a) für morgen
   b) für nächsten Monat
   c) für das Jahr 1985!
2. Glauben Sie an Astrologie? Warum? Warum nicht?
3. Spielen Sie die Rollen von Handleser/Handleserin (palm-reader) und Kunden. Gebrauchen Sie viel Phantasie dabei!

168

DAS WETTER

18

Das Wetter spielt eine große Rolle in unserem Leben. Solange es gut ist, reden wir nicht sehr viel darüber. Aber in dem Moment, in dem Regen, Sturm oder Gewitter aufziehen, kann das Wetter für uns zu einer Gefahr werden. Obwohl es in Deutschland keine Hurrikane oder Tornados gibt, können Stürme Häuser abdecken und die Bäume ganzer Wälder umknicken. Damit wir uns vor diesen Unwettern besser schützen können, gibt es die Wettervorhersagen. Wettervorhersagen sind in Europa für die Landwirtschaft und Schiffahrt wichtig, außerdem für Freizeit und Verkehr.

Jedes Land hat mehrere Wetterämter. Die Leute, die dort arbeiten, heißen Meteorologen; sie beobachten den ganzen Tag das Wetter und sammeln Meßdaten. Ihre Beobachtungen tragen sie in eine Wetterkarte ein. Jeden Tag können wir im Radio darüber hören und im Fernsehen oder in der Zeitung die Wetterkarten sehen. Auf diesen Karten gibt es verschiedene Zeichen für den Luftdruck, die Temperatur, den Wind und den Regen.

Ein großes „H" ist die Abkürzung für Hochdruckgebiet. Ein Hochdruckgebiet bringt im Sommer schönes Wetter und im Winter meistens Frost, denn ein Wettergebiet mit hohem Luftdruck hat wenig Wolken. Der Gegensatz dazu ist ein Tiefdruckgebiet. Es wird mit einem „T" gekennzeichnet. Ein Tiefdruckgebiet ist immer ein Zeichen für schlechtes Wetter.

Die Temperatur der Luft messen wir mit einem Thermometer. Auf einem Barometer können wir ablesen, ob es gutes oder schlechtes Wetter geben wird. Ein Barometer mißt nämlich den Luftdruck.

Die Wettervorhersagen sind seit der Erfindung der Satelliten immer genauer geworden. Wettersatelliten, die um die Erde kreisen, fotografieren Wolkendecken. Mit Hilfe dieser Fotografien können die Meteorologen ziemlich genau feststellen, wie schnell die Wettergebiete sich um unsere Erdkugel bewegen. Braut sich ein Wirbelsturm zusammen, so können die Leute in den bedrohten Landesteilen rechtzeitig davor gewarnt werden.

WORTSCHATZ

die Abkürzung, -en *abbreviation*
das Barometer, - *barometer*
die Beobachtung, -en *observation*
die Erfindung, -en *discovery*
die Fotografie, -n *photograph*
der Frost, ¨e *frost*
die Gefahr, -en *danger*
der Gegensatz, ¨e *opposite*
das Gewitter, - *thunderstorm*
das Hochdruckgebiet, -e *high pressure area*
der Hurrikan, -e *hurricane*
der Luftdruck *air pressure*
die Meßdaten (pl.) *measurement data*
der Meteorologe, -n *meteorologist*
der Regen *rain*
der Satellit, -en *satellite*
der Sturm, ¨e *storm*
die Temperatur, -en *temperature*
das Thermometer, - *thermometer*
das Tiefdruckgebiet, -e *low pressure area*
der Tornado, -s *tornado*
das Unwetter, - *bad weather*
das Wetter *weather*
das Wetteramt, ¨er *weather bureau*
das Wettergebiet, -e *weather area*
die Wettervorhersage, -n *weather forecast*
die Wetterkarte, -n *weather map*
der Wind, -e *wind*

die Wolke, -n *cloud*
die Wolkendecke, -n *cloud cover*
das Zeichen, - *symbol, sign*

ab·decken *to uncover, unroof*
auf·ziehen, zog auf, ist aufgezogen *to arise (storms), to bring up (children)*
beobachten *to observe*
ein·tragen (trägt ein), trug ein, eingetragen *to enter (in a ledger)*
fest·stellen *to determine*
fotografieren *to photograph*
kennzeichnen *to mark, designate*
kreisen *to circle*
messen (mißt), maß, gemessen *to measure*
sammeln *to gather*
schützen vor (+ dat.) *to protect from*
um·knicken *to snap off*
warnen vor (+ dat.) *to warn of*
sich zusammen·brauen *to brew together (storms)*

bedroht *threatened*
meistens *mostly*
nämlich *namely*
rechtzeitig *prompt(ly)*
ziemlich *rather, pretty much*

im Radio, im Fernsehen *on the radio, on television*
in dem Moment *at the moment*

ZUM BESPRECHEN

1. Wieso sind Wettervorhersagen wertvoll?
2. Was machen die Meteorologen?
3. Was für Wetter bringt ein Hochdruckgebiet? Ein Tiefdruckgebiet?
4. Beschreiben Sie den Unterschied zwischen einem Thermometer und einem Barometer.
5. Warum sind Wettersatelliten für die Meteorologen wichtig?

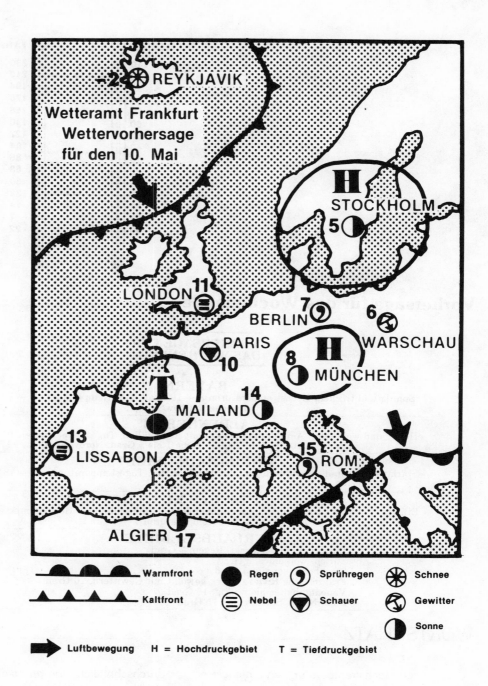

Warmfront · Regen · Sprühregen · Schnee

Kaltfront · Nebel · Schauer · Gewitter

Sonne

➡ Luftbewegung   H = Hochdruckgebiet   T = Tiefdruckgebiet

WORTSCHATZ

die Kaltfront, -en *cold front*

die Luftbewegung, -en *air movement*

der Nebel *fog*

der Schauer, - *showers*

der Schnee *snow*

der Sprühregen *drizzle*

die Warmfront, -en *warm front*

171

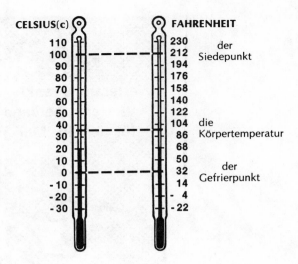

CELSIUS(c)	FAHRENHEIT	
110	230	der
100	212	Siedepunkt
90	194	
80	176	
70	158	
60	140	
50	122	
40	104	die
30	86	Körpertemperatur
20	68	
10	50	
0	32	der
-10	14	Gefrierpunkt
-20	- 4	
-30	- 22	

Vorhersage für das Wochenende

VORHERSAGE FÜR DAS WOCHENENDE

BAYERN
Sonnig und trocken. Höchsttemperaturen 8 — 10 Grad. Tiefsttemperaturen 5 — 7 Grad. Schwache Luftbewegung.

ALPENGEBIET
Heiter und wolkenlos. Am Sonntag wolkig mit Regenfällen. Tagestemperaturen 10 — 11, nachts 5 — 10 Grad. In 2000 m Höhe 1 bis 5 Grad. Nordwestwind.

RHEIN-MAIN-GEBIET
Stark bewölkt und zeitweise Regenfälle und Gewitter. Tagestemperaturen 12 — 18 Grad, nachts 10 — 7 Grad.

NORDDEUTSCHES KÜSTENGEBIET
Einzelne Schauer oder Gewitter. Am Sonntag Nebel und Sprühregen. Höchsttemperaturen 7 — 10 Grad. Tiefsttemperaturen 4 — 7 Grad.

URLAUBSGEBIETE
Innsbruck: fast bedeckt, Regen, 7 Grad
Zürich: wolkenlos, 8 Grad
Stockholm: sonnig, 5 Grad
Französische Riviera: stark bewölkt mit Gewittern, 20 Grad
Venedig: heiter bis wolkig, 18 Grad
Rom: Nebel, Sprühregen, 15 Grad

WORTSCHATZ

die Höchsttemperatur, -en *highest temperature*
das Küstengebiet, -e *coastal area*
der Regenfall, ⸚e *rainfall, precipitation*
die Tagestemperatur, -en *daytime temperature*
die Tiefsttemperatur, -en *lowest temperature*

bedeckt *overcast*
bewölkt *cloudy, overcast*

durchschnittlich *on an average*
einzeln *single, isolated*
heiter *clear, bright*
schwach *weak, mild*
sonnig *sunny*
stark *strong, heavily*
trocken *dry*
wolkenlos *cloudless*
wolkig *cloudy*
zeitweise *at times, from time to time*

ZUM BESPRECHEN

1. Sehen Sie sich die Wetterkarte an. Machen Sie eine Wettervorhersage für a) London b) Stockholm c) München d) Paris e) Berlin f) Warschau g) Reykjavik.
2. Wird das Wetter in den nächsten Tagen in England und in Griechenland wärmer oder kälter? Woher wissen Sie das?
3. Wo wird das Wetter in Deutschland am schönsten sein? Warum?
4. Sie wollen in den Urlaub fahren. Wo müssen Sie hinfahren, um das schönste Wetter zu haben?
5. Sie fahren nach Lissabon. Welche Kleidung sollten Sie für das Wochenende mitnehmen?
6. Sind die Temperaturen im Mai in Europa durchschnittlich höher oder tiefer als in Ihrem Staat?

ZUR AUSFÜHRLICHEN DISKUSSION

1. Ein Bekannter, der in den USA wohnt, fährt nächste Woche nach München. Erklären Sie ihm die Wetterlage in Deutschland.
2. Kann man der Wettervorhersage immer trauen? Warum oder warum nicht?
3. Mögen Sie kaltes oder warmes Wetter lieber? Warum?
4. Welche Jahreszeit (Frühling, Sommer, Herbst, oder Winter) ist Ihnen am liebsten? Warum?
5. Beschreiben Sie den schlimmsten Sturm, den Sie je erlebt haben.
6. Zeichnen Sie eine Wetterkarte Ihres Staates (oder der USA) an die Tafel. Lesen Sie Ihre Wettervorhersage für das Wochenende vor. Beantworten Sie mögliche Fragen Ihrer Kommilitonen.

ZUM BESPRECHEN

1. Welche Jahreszeiten sind auf den Bildern dargestellt? Beschreiben Sie jeweils das Wetter.
2. Was machen die Menschen auf den vier Bildern?
3. Beschreiben Sie die Kleidung der Leute.
4. In welche Bilder möchten Sie sich hineinversetzen? Warum?

Metric Equivalents

Length:

1 inch = 25.4 millimeters, 2.54 centimeters	1 millimeter = 0.039 inch
1 foot = 30.48 centimeters	1 centimeter = 0.39 inch
1 yard = 91.44 centimeters	1 meter = 39.37 inches
1 mile = 1.6 kilometers	1 kilometer = 0.62 mile

Height:

5'0" = 1m 52 cm	5'5" = 1m 65 cm	5' 9" = 1m 75 cm
5'1" = 1m 55 cm	5'6" = 1m 68 cm	5'10" = 1m 78 cm
5'2" = 1m 57 cm	5'7" = 1m 70 cm	5'11" = 1m 80 cm
5'3" = 1m 60 cm	5'8" = 1m 73 cm	6' 0" = 1m 83 cm
5'4" = 1m 62 cm		

Distance:

10 miles = 16 km	25 miles = 40 km	1 km = .621 miles
12.4 miles = 20 km	62 miles = 100 km	1 mile = 1.6 km

Weight:

1 ounce = 28.3 grams	1 gram = 0.035 ounce
1 pound = 454 grams, 0.45 kilogram	1 kilogram = 2.2 pounds

* * *

100 lbs = 45.4 kg	120 lbs = 54.5 kg	140 lbs = 63.6 kg
110 lbs = 49.9 kg	130 lbs = 59.0 kg	150 lbs = 68.1 kg

160 lbs = 72.6 kg   180 lbs = 81.7 kg   200 lbs = 90.8 kg
170 lbs = 77.2 kg   190 lbs = 86.3 kg

Liquid Measure:

1 pint   = 0.47 liter   1 liter = 2.13 pints, 1.064 quarts, 0.26 U.S. gallon
1 quart = 0.95 liter
1 gallon = 3.79 liters

Temperature:

1 degree Centigrade = 1.8 degree Fahrenheit
1 degree Fahrenheit = 0.55 degree Centigrade

FAHRENHEIT	CENTIGRADE	FAHRENHEIT	CENTIGRADE
212	100	32	0
104	40	30	−1
100	38	20	−7
98.6	37	10	−12
90	32	0	−18
80	27	−10	−23
70	21	−20	−29
60	15	−30	−34
50	10	−40	−40
40	4		

Principal Parts of Strong Verbs

INFINITIVE	THIRD PERSON SINGULAR PRESENT	FIRST AND THIRD PERSON SINGULAR PAST	PAST PARTICIPLE	
backen	bäckt	buk (backte)	gebacken (gebackt)	to bake
befehlen	befiehlt	befahl	befohlen	to command
beginnen	beginnt	begann	begonnen	to begin
beißen	beißt	biß	gebissen	to bite
bersten	birst	barst	ist geborsten	to burst
betrügen	betrügt	betrog	betrogen	to deceive

INFINITIVE	THIRD PERSON SINGULAR PRESENT	FIRST AND THIRD PERSON SINGULAR PAST	PAST PARTICIPLE	
biegen	biegt	bog	ist hat } gebogen	to turn; bend
bieten	bietet	bot	geboten	to offer
binden	bindet	band	gebunden	to tie, bind
bitten	bittet	bat	gebeten	to request
bleiben	bleibt	blieb	ist geblieben	to remain
brechen	bricht	brach	gebrochen	to break
brennen	brennt	brannte	gebrannt	to burn
bringen	bringt	brachte	gebracht	to bring
denken	denkt	dachte	gedacht	to think
dringen	dringt	drang	ist gedrungen	to force a way, burst forth, press
empfehlen	empfiehlt	empfahl	empfohlen	to recommend
entringen	entringt	entrang	entrungen	to wrest from
erheben	erhebt	erhob	erhoben	to raise, elevate
erscheinen	erscheint	erschien	ist erschienen	to appear
erschrecken	erschrickt	erschrak	ist erschrocken	to be startled, frightened
erwerben	erwirbt	erwarb	erworben	to acquire, gain, earn
essen	ißt	aß	gegessen	to eat
fahren	fährt	fuhr	ist hat } gefahren	to ride, travel, go; drive
fallen	fällt	fiel	ist gefallen	to fall
fangen	fängt	fing	gefangen	to catch
fechten	ficht	focht	gefochten	to fight, duel
finden	findet	fand	gefunden	to find
fliegen	fliegt	flog	ist hat } geflogen	to fly
fliehen	flieht	floh	ist geflohen	to flee
fließen	fließt	floß	ist geflossen	to flow
fressen	frißt	fraß	gefressen	to eat (refers to animals' eating)
frieren	friert	fror	gefroren	to freeze, be cold
gebären	gebärt	gebar	geboren	to give birth to
geben	gibt	gab	gegeben	to give
gedeihen	gedeiht	gedieh	ist gediehen	to flourish, thrive
gehen	geht	ging	ist gegangen	to go
gelingen	gelingt	gelang	ist gelungen	to succeed
gelten	gilt	galt	gegolten	to apply, be worth, have value, be valid
genießen	genießt	genoß	genossen	to enjoy
geschehen	geschieht	geschah	ist geschehen	to happen
gewinnen	gewinnt	gewann	gewonnen	to obtain, win, acquire
gießen	gießt	goß	gegossen	to pour
gleichen	gleicht	glich	geglichen	to be equal to; resemble
gleiten	gleitet	glitt	ist geglitten	to glide, slip
graben	gräbt	grub	gegraben	to dig

177

INFINITIVE	THIRD PERSON SINGULAR PRESENT	FIRST AND THIRD PERSON SINGULAR PAST		PAST PARTICIPLE	
greifen	greift	griff		gegriffen	*to seize*
halten	hält	hielt		gehalten	*to stop, halt; hold*
hängen	hängt	hing		gehangen	*to hang*
heben	hebt	hob		gehoben	*to lift*
heißen	heißt	hieß		geheißen	*to be called*
helfen	hilft	half		geholfen	*to help*
kennen	kennt	kannte		gekannt	*to know*
klingen	klingt	klang		geklungen	*to sound*
kommen	kommt	kam	ist	gekommen	*to come*
kriechen	kriecht	kroch	ist	gekrochen	*to creep*
lassen	läßt	ließ		gelassen	*to leave, let, allow, cause*
laufen	läuft	lief	ist	gelaufen	*to run*
leiden	leidet	litt		gelitten	*to suffer*
leihen	leiht	lieh		geliehen	*to lend; borrow*
lesen	liest	las		gelesen	*to read*
liegen	liegt	lag		gelegen	*to lie, be situated*
lügen	lügt	log		gelogen	*to tell a lie*
nehmen	nimmt	nahm		genommen	*to take*
nennen	nennt	nannte		genannt	*to name, call*
raten	rät	riet		geraten	*to advise*
reißen	reißt	riß	ist⎫hat⎭	gerissen	*to tear*
reiten	reitet	ritt	ist⎫hat⎭	geritten	*to ride*
rennen	rennt	rannte	ist	gerannt	*to run*
riechen	riecht	roch		gerochen	*to smell*
rufen	ruft	rief		gerufen	*to call*
saufen	säuft	soff		gesoffen	*to drink (refers to animals' drinking)*
scheiden	scheidet	schied	ist⎫hat⎭	geschieden	*to depart; separate*
scheinen	scheint	schien		geschienen	*to seem, appear, shine*
schießen	schießt	schoß		geschossen	*to shoot*
schlafen	schläft	schlief		geschlafen	*to sleep*
schlagen	schlägt	schlug		geschlagen	*to hit, strike, beat*
schleichen	schleicht	schlich	ist	geschlichen	*to sneak*
schließen	schließt	schloß		geschlossen	*to close*
schneiden	schneidet	schnitt		geschnitten	*to cut*
schreiben	schreibt	schrieb		geschrieben	*to write*
schreien	schreit	schrie		geschrie(e)n	*to cry, scream*
schreiten	schreitet	schritt	ist	geschritten	*to stride, walk*
schweigen	schweigt	schwieg		geschwiegen	*to be silent*
schwimmen	schwimmt	schwamm	ist⎫hat⎭	geschwommen	*to swim*
schwingen	schwingt	schwang		geschwungen	*to swing, vibrate*

INFINITIVE	THIRD PERSON SINGULAR PRESENT	FIRST AND THIRD PERSON SINGULAR PAST		PAST PARTICIPLE	
sehen	sieht	sah		gesehen	to see
senden	sendet	sandte		gesandt	to send
singen	singt	sang		gesungen	to sing
sinken	sinkt	sank	ist	gesunken	to sink
sprechen	spricht	sprach		gesprochen	to speak
springen	springt	sprang	ist	gesprungen	to jump
stechen	sticht	stach		gestochen	to pierce; sting
stehen	steht	stand		gestanden	to stand
stehlen	stiehlt	stahl		gestohlen	to steal
steigen	steigt	stieg	ist	gestiegen	to climb
sterben	stirbt	starb	ist	gestorben	to die
stinken	stinkt	stank		gestunken	to stink
stoßen	stößt	stieß	ist hat	gestoßen	to push, strike
tragen	trägt	trug		getragen	to carry; wear
treffen	trifft	traf		getroffen	to meet; hit
treiben	treibt	trieb	ist hat	getrieben	to drift; drive, carry on
treten	tritt	trat	ist hat	getreten	to step, walk; enter; kick
trinken	trinkt	trank		getrunken	to drink
tun	tut	tat		getan	to do
überwinden	überwindet	überwand		überwunden	to overcome, surmount
unterstreichen	unterstreicht	unterstrich		unterstrichen	to underline
verbergen	verbirgt	verbarg		verborgen	to hide
verderben	verdirbt	verdarb		verdorben	to ruin
vergessen	vergißt	vergaß		vergessen	to forget
verleihen	verleiht	verlieh		verliehen	to give, bestow
verlieren	verliert	verlor		verloren	to lose
verschlingen	verschlingt	verschlang		verschlungen	to swallow, consume
verschwinden	verschwindet	verschwand	ist	verschwunden	to disappear
wachsen	wächst	wuchs	ist	gewachsen	to grow
waschen	wäscht	wusch		gewaschen	to wash
weisen	weist	wies		gewiesen	to indicate, point out
wenden	wendet	wandte		gewandt	to turn
werfen	wirft	warf		geworfen	to throw
wiegen	wiegt	wog		gewogen	to weigh
ziehen	zieht	zog	ist hat	gezogen	to move; pull, draw
zwingen	zwingt	zwang		gezwungen	to force

Wörterverzeichnis

Nouns

Nouns are listed with (1) the definite article, and (2) the formation of the plural. "–" indicates no change in the formation of the plural:

der Bäcker, –.

Masculine nouns followed by **-en** or **-n** require those endings in all cases, including the singular and plural, except in the nominative singular:

der Architekt -en, -en
der Student, -en, -en

In normal usage no plurals exist for many nouns:

der Apfelsaft
die Armut
die Kunsterziehung
die Musik

Nouns that behave like adjectives in regard to their endings are listed in the following manner:

der Beamte, –n, –n (ein Beamter)

Verbs

Weak verbs are given only in the infinitive.
The principal parts of strong verbs are listed as follows:

lassen (läßt), ließ, gelassen
geschehen (geschieht), geschah, ist geschehen

Separable prefix verbs are separated by a dot:

ab·lehnen
um·ziehen, zog·um, ist umgezogen

180

Abbreviations

The following abbreviations have been used:

acc.	accusative	*fem.*	feminine
colloq.	colloquial	*gen.*	genitive
conj.	conjunction	*masc.*	masculine
dat.	dative	*pl.*	plural

A

ab·decken to uncover; unroof

der **Abend, -e** evening

abends in the evening

ab·fahren (fährt ab), fuhr ab, ist abgefahren to leave, depart

die **Abfahrtzeit, -en** time of departure

ab·heben, hob ab, abgehoben to lift up or off; **Geld ab·heben** to withdraw money from a bank

ab·holen to pick up

das **Abitur, -e** examination given at the end of the secondary school (the **Gymnasium**) qualifying for admission to the university

die **Abkürzung, -en** abbreviation

ab·lehnen to refuse

ab·lesen (liest ab), las ab, abgelesen to read off

sich **ab·melden** to check out (of a hotel)

ab·schließen, schloß ab, abgeschlossen to conclude

der **Abschluß, -sse** diploma

ab·stellen to turn or shut off

die **Abteilung, -en** department

der **Abteilungsleiter, –** department chairman or director

die **Abwechslung** variety

die **Abwesenheit, -en** absence

achten auf *(+ acc.)* to pay attention to

die **Ächtung** outlawing

die **Adresse, -n** address

ähnlich similar

die **Ähnlichkeit, -en** similarity

akademisch academic

das **Album, -ben** album

allein alone

allemal always

allerdings of course

alltäglich everyday

der **Amerikaner, –** American *(masc.)*

die **Amerikanerin, -nen** American *(fem.)*

die **Amerikanistik** American studies

an·bieten, bot an, angeboten to offer

der **Anfang, -e** beginning

an·fangen (fängt an) fing an, angefangen to begin

der **Anfänger, –** beginner

die **Angaben** *(pl.)* details, data

an·geben, gab an, angegeben to state, indicate

das **Angebot, -e** offer

angeheitert tipsy, "mellow"

angeln to fish

angenehm pleasant

der **Angestellte, -n, -n (ein Angestellter)** employee (salaried)

anhand *(+ gen.)* with the aid of

an·hören to listen to

der **Ankauf, -e** purchase

an·kommen, kam an, ist angekommen to arrive

an·kreuzen to check

die **Ankunftzeit, -en** time of arrival

an·lassen (läßt an), ließ an, angelassen to start (an engine), to turn on (water)

an·machen to fasten, fix, attach; **einen Salat an·machen** to dress a salad

das **Anmeldeformular, (-e)** registration form

sich **an·melden** to announce oneself; register; check in

an·nehmen (nimmt an), nahm an, angenommen to accept

an·probieren to try on

an·reden to address, speak to

an·rufen, rief an, angerufen to call up, telephone

sich **etwas** *(acc.)* **anschauen** to look at something; **sich eine Fernsehsendung anschauen** to watch a TV program

anscheinend apparently

anschließend afterwards

sich **an·schnallen** to buckle one's seat belt

die **Anschrift, -en** address

an·sehen (sieht an), sah an, angesehen to look at; **sich etwas** *(acc.)* **ansehen** to look at something

die **Ansicht, -en** viewpoint

die **Ansichtskarte, -n** picture postcard

anspruchsvoll exacting, demanding

an·starren to stare at

an·stellen to hire

sich **an·stellen** to stand in line

an·stoßen (stößt an), stieß an, angestoßen to clink glasses as a toast; **auf deine Gesundheit anstoßen** to drink to your health

die **Antenne, -en** antenna

die **Anzahl** number

an·zahlen to make a down payment

die **Anzahlung, -en** down payment

die **Anzeige, -en** advertisement

der **Anzug, -e** suit

an·zünden to light, ignite

apart attractive, special

der **Apfel, –** apple

der **Apfelsaft** apple juice

die **Apotheke, -n** drug store

181

das **Appartement, -s** suite of rooms, efficiency apartment

arbeiten to work; **arbeiten an** (+ acc.) to work on

der **Arbeiter, –** worker

die **Arbeiterin, -nen** worker (fem.)

das **Arbeitsamt, ⸚er** employment agency

der **Arbeitsplatz, ⸚e** job

das **Arbeitszimmer, –** study

der **Architekt, -en, -en** architect

sich **ärgern über** (+ acc.) to get annoyed at

das **Argument, -e** argument

der **Arm, -e** arm

das **Armband, ⸚er** bracelet

die **Armut** poverty

die **Art, -en** type, kind

der **Artikel, –** article

der **Arzt, ⸚e** physician (masc.)

die **Ärztin, -nen** physician (fem.)

der **Aspekt, -e** aspect

die **Atmosphäre, -n** atmosphere

auf einmal at once, immediately

die **Aufgabe, -n** task; lesson

auf·geben (gibt auf), gab auf, aufgegeben to give up; **einen Brief, ein Paket aufgeben** to mail a letter, a package

aufgeschlossen open, accessible

auf·lösen to dissolve

auf·nehmen (nimmt auf), nahm auf, aufgenommen to take in, admit; **ein Foto aufnehmen** to take a photo

auf·stehen, stand auf, ist aufgestanden to get up

auf·teilen to divide up

auf·wachen, ist aufgewacht to wake up

auf·ziehen, zog auf, ist aufgezogen to arise (storms), bring up (children)

das **Auge, -n** eye

die **Auseinandersetzung, -en** argument

ausführlich in detail, fully

aus·füllen to fill out

ausgestattet equipped

der **Ausguß, ⸚sse** sink

aus·knipsen to turn off

die **Auskunft, ⸚e** information

das **Ausland** foreign country, abroad

ausländisch foreign

der **Auspuff, -e** exhaust

ausreichend adequate

das **Aussehen** appearance

aus·sehen (sieht aus), sah aus, ausgesehen to look, appear

außen outside

die **Außenpolitik** foreign policy

der **Außenseiter –** outsider

außerdem besides, moreover

die **Ausstattung** accessory package

aus·steigen, stieg aus, ist ausgestiegen to get off, disembark

aus·suchen to choose, select

aus·üben to carry out, execute; **einen Beruf ausüben** to practice a profession

der **Ausverkauf** sale (prices reduced)

aus·wählen to select

das **Auswahlessen, –** meal in university "Mensa" where student can select from choices available

der **Ausweis, -e** license

das **Auto, -s** automobile

das **Autofahren** driving

der **Autohändler, –** auto dealer

die **Autokenntnisse** (pl.) knowledge of cars

automatisch automatic

der **Automechaniker, –** auto mechanic

der **Autoverleih, -e** auto rental company

das **Autozubehör** auto-accessories

B

backen(bäckt), backte, gebacken to bake

der **Bäcker, –** baker

die **Bäckerei, -en** bakery

der **Backofen, ⸚** oven

das **Backpulver** baking powder

das **Bad, ⸚er** bath

der **Badeanzug, ⸚e** bathing suit

baden to bathe

die **Badewanne, -n** bathtub

die **Bahn, -en** railroad; **mit der Bahn fahren** to travel by train

der **Bahnhof, ⸚e** railroad station

der **Bahnsteig, -e** railway platform

bald soon

der **Balkon, -e** balcony

die **Banane, -n** banana

die **Bank, ⸚e** bench

der **Bankier, -s** banker

das **Bargeld** cash

das **Barometer, –** barometer

basteln to work with metal, paper, or wood as a hobby

die **Batterie, -n** battery

der **Batteriebetrieb, -e** battery operation

der **Bauer, -n** farmer (masc.)

die **Bäuerin, -nen** farmer (fem.)

das **Baujahr, -e** year of construction

die **Baumwollwaren** (pl.) cottons

der **Beamte, -n, -n (ein Beamter)** civil servant, official

beaufsichtigen to watch, supervise
der **Becher, –** mug
bedeckt overcast
bedeuten to mean
bedeutungslos meaningless
die **Bedienung** service, table service
die **Bedingung, -en** requirement
die **Bedrängnis** trouble, distress
bedrohen to threaten
beenden to finish, conclude
sich **befassen (mit)** to occupy oneself (with)
sich **befinden, befand sich, sich befund-en** to be located
befragen to ask
befriedigend satisfactory
der **Beginn** beginning
beginnen, begann, begonnen to begin
begründen to prove, give reasons for
die **Behörde, -n** local government
bei·bringen (+ *dat.*) to teach
das **Beispiel, -e** example
beispielsweise for example
der **Beistelltisch, -e** side table
die **Bekanntschaft, -en** acquaintance
das **Bekenntnis, -se** confession; (religious) denomination
beklagen to complain, lament; **sich beklagen bei jemandem über etwas** (*acc.*) to complain to someone about something
bekommen, bekam, bekommen to get, receive
beladen (belädt), belud, beladen to load
belegen to cover, line
Belgien Belgium
belügen, belog, belogen to lie, to deceive by lying
bemerken to notice
sich **bemühen** to try, endeavor
sich **benehmen (benimmt sich), benahm sich, sich benommen** to behave
benennen, benannte, benannt to name
benutzen to use
das **Benzin** gasoline
der **Benzindurst** (*colloq.*) gas consumption ("thirst")
beobachten to observe
die **Beobachtung, -en** observation
bequem comfortable
der **Berater, –** adviser
die **Berechnung, -en** calculation, account
berechtigen to entitle, justify
berechtigt justified
bereit ready
bereits already

das **Bergsteigen** mountain climbing
berichten to report
der **Beruf, -e** profession, occupation
die **Berufsausbildung, -en** education for a profession
die **Berufsberatungsstelle, -n** job advisement service
die **Berufserfahrung, -en** occupational experience
die **Berufslaufbahn, -en** career
die **Berufsmöglichkeit, -en** career possibility
die **Berufsschule, -n** vocational school
die **Berufswahl, -en** choice of career
berühmt famous
sich **beschäftigen mit** to be busy with
die **Beschäftigung, -en** employment
Bescheid wissen to know what's going on
beschreiben, beschrieb, beschrieben to describe
die **Beschreibung, -en** description
besitzen, besaß, besessen to own, possess
der **Besitzer, –** owner
besonders especially
besprechen (bespricht), besprach, besprochen to discuss
bestäuben to sprinkle, dust
das **Besteck, -e** cutlery, silverware
bestellen to order
bestimmt certain, definite
der **Besuch, -e** attendance; visit, company
besuchen to visit
die **Betätigung, -en** activity
betrachten to look at, examine
der **Betrag, ⸚e** amount, sum, total; **die Beträge zusammen·zählen** to add up the bill
betragen (beträgt), betrug, betragen to come to, amount to; **Wieviel beträgt meine Rechnung?** What does my bill come to?
betreten (betritt), betrat, betreten to enter
die **Betreuung** care and control
der **Betrieb, -e** activity, bustle; operation
die **Betriebskosten** (*pl.*) maintenance expenses
sich **betrinken, betrank sich, sich betrunken** to get drunk
betrügen, betrog, betrogen to deceive
das **Bett, -en** bed; **ins Bett gehen** to go to bed
der **Bettbezug, ⸚e** bed linen
das **Bettuch, ⸚er** sheet
die **Bettwaren** (*pl.*) bed articles

183

die **Bettwäsche** bed linen
beurteilen to evaluate
bevölkert populated
die **Bevölkerung, -en** population
bevorzugen to prefer
beweisen, bewies, bewiesen to prove
sich **bewerben (bewirbt sich), bewarb sich, sich beworben** to apply, seek; **sich bewerben um** to apply for
der **Bewerber, –** applicant
die **Bewerbung, -en** application
bewölkt cloudy, overcast
bewundern to admire
bezahlen to pay
die **Bezahlung** pay
bezeichnen to designate, characterize
die **Beziehung, -en** relationship
die **Bibliothek, -en** library
das **Bier, -e** beer; **ein "Bierchen" trinken gehen** to go for a beer
der **Bierkeller, –** pub
bieten, bot, geboten to offer
das **Bild, -er** picture, photograph
bildhübsch extremely pretty
die **Bildung** education
die **Bildungslektüre** educational literature
die **Bildzuschrift, -en** letter with photo
billig inexpensive
die **Biologie** biology
bitter bitter
blau blue; drunk (colloq.)
das **Blaukraut** red cabbage
der **Blechschaden, ⸚** body damage (of cars)
der **Bleistift, -e** pencil
der **Blick, -e** look, glance
das **Blinklicht, -er** directional signal
der **Blitz, -e** lightning flash
die **Bockwurst, ⸚e** bockwurst
der **Boden, ⸚** floor
die **Bombe, -n** bomb
das **Bord, -e** shelf, board
der **Braten, –** roast
braten (brät), briet, gebraten to roast
die **Bratwurst, ⸚e** fried sausage
brauchen to need
brauen to brew
der **Brauer, –** brewer
die **Brausetablette, -n** effervescent tablet
das **Brautkleid, -er** bridal gown
der **Brei** broth; hot cereal
die **Bremse, -n** brake
brennen, brannte, gebrannt to burn
das **Brett, -er** board; **das schwarze Brett** bulletin board
die **Brezel, -n** pretzel

der **Brief, -e** letter
der **Briefkasten, ⸚** mail box
die **Briefmarke, -n** stamp
der **Briefumschlag, ⸚e** envelope
die **Brille, -n** glasses
das **Brillengeschäft, -e** optician
bringen, brachte, gebracht to bring
die **Brotzeit** (Bavarian and Austrian expression) between-meal snack
der **Bruder, ⸚** brother
die **Brühpolnisch** Polish sausage
brünett brunette
das **Buch, ⸚er** book
das **Bücherregal, -e** bookshelf, bookstack
die **Buchhandlung, -en** book store
büffeln to cram, study hard
das **Buffet, -s** buffet, snack bar
Bulgarien Bulgaria
die **Bundesrepublik Deutschland (BRD)** Federal Republic of Germany
bunt colorful, bright
der **Bürgermeister, –** mayor
der **Bürgersteig, -e** sidewalk
das **Büro, -s** office
der **Bus, -se** bus
die **Butter** butter

C

das **Café, -s** café
der **Cartoon, -s** cartoon
die **Chance, -n** chance
der **Chef, -s** boss
die **Chemie** chemistry
chronisch chronic
die **City, -s** center city
das **Cola, -s** cola
der **Computer, –** computer
die **Computerwissenschaft, -en** computer science
der **Couchtisch, -e** coffee table
das **Curriculum** curriculum
die **Currywurst, ⸚e** curry sausage

D

dabei sein to be there, to be present
das **Dach, ⸚er** roof
die **Dachrinne, -n** gutter
die **Damenbekleidung** women's clothing
die **Damenboutique, -en** women's boutique
die **Damenwäsche** lingerie
damit (conj.) so that
das **Dämmerlicht** twilight
der **Däne, -n** Dane (masc.)
Dänemark Denmark

die **Dänin, -nen** Dane *(fem.)*
dänisch Danish
dar·stellen to represent, depict
das **Datum, -ten** date
dauern to last
die **Dauerstellung, -en** long–term position
dazu in addition to; to it or for it
die **Decke, -n** blanket
decken to cover; **den Tisch decken** to set the table
die **Demokratie, -n** democracy
denken, dachte, gedacht to think; **denken an** *(+ acc.)* to think of
sich **denken, dachte sich, sich gedacht** *(dat.)* to think to oneself
deshalb therefore
das **Detail, -s** detail
detonieren to detonate
deutsch German; **das Deutsch** German language; **auf deutsch** in German; **der Deutsche, -n, -n;** German native *(masc.);* **die Deutsche, -n** German native *(fem.);* **die Deutsche Mark (DM)** German mark
die **Deutsche Demokratische Republik (DDR)** German Democratic Republic (East Germany)
(das) **Deutschland** Germany
deutschsprachig German-speaking
dicht thick, dense, close
dick fat, thick
die **Diebstahlsicherung, -en** anti-theft device
der **Dienst, -e** service
das **Diktaphon -e** dictaphone
der **Diktator, -en** dictator
die **Diktatur, -en** dictatorship
das **Ding, -e** thing
der **Discjockey, -s** disk jockey
die **Diskothek, -en** discothèque
die **Diskussion, -en** discussion
das **Doppelzimmer, –** double room
das **Dorf, ̈er** village
dreijährig three-year
dringend urgent
drittens thirdly
drohen *(+ dat.)* to threaten
der **Drückeberger, –** work-shirker
drücken to press
dunkelblau dark blue
durchgehend continuously
durchsichtig transparent
die **Dusche, -n** shower
sich **duschen** to take a shower
die **Düsseldorferin, -nen** woman from Düsseldorf

E _____

ebenso wie as well as
echt genuine
die **Ecke, -n** corner
eheähnlich quasi–marital
die **Ehre** honor, respect
ehrlich honest
das **Ei, -er** egg
eifrig ambitious
das **Eigelb, -e** egg yolk
eigen own, individual
die **Eigenschaft, -en** quality
eigentlich real, actual
die **Eigentumswohnung,-en** condominium
sich **eignen (zu)** to be suitable (for)
einander one another
ein·atmen to inhale
die **Einbahnstraße, -n** one-way street
der **Einbauschrank, ̈e** closet
das **Einbettzimmer, –** single room
einfach simple
Einfahrt verboten! Do not enter!
der **Einfluß, ̈sse** influence
die **Einführung, -en** introduction
einigermaßen to some extent
das **Einkaufen** shopping; **beim Einkaufen** when shopping
ein·kaufen to shop; **einkaufen gehen** to go shopping
der **Einkäufer, –** purchaser
die **Einkaufstasche, -n** shopping bag
der **Einkaufswagen, –** shopping cart
das **Einkaufszentrum, -tren** shopping center
das **Einkommen, –** income
ein·legen to put in, insert; **eine Pause einlegen** to take a break
ein·nehmen (nimmt ein), nahm ein, eingenommen to take (medicine)
ein·packen to wrap up, pack
ein·richten to set up, arrange; to furnish
die **Einrichtung, -en** accomodation, furnishing
einsam lonely
die **Einsatzfreude** initiative
einsatzfreudig initiating, ready to go
ein·schlagen (schlägt ein), schlug ein, eingeschlagen to strike
ein·schließen, schloß ein, eingeschlossen to include
einschließlich inclusive
die **Einschreibegebühr, -en** registration fee
ein·schreiben, schrieb ein, eingeschrieben to register; **einen Brief**

185

einschreiben lassen to register a letter

ein·steigen, stieg ein, eingestiegen to get on, board

das **Einstellungsgespräch, ⸚e** job interview; **ein Einstellungsgespräch führen** to conduct a job interview

ein·tauschen to exchange

ein·tragen (trägt ein), trug ein, eingetragen to enter (in a ledger)

einwandfrei mint condition

ein·weihen to dedicate

ein·werfen (wirft ein), warf ein, eingeworfen to deposit, insert; **einen Brief einwerfen** to drop a letter into a mailbox

der **Einwohner, –** resident

einzeln single, individual

das **Einzelzimmer, –** single room

das **Eis** ice cream

das **Eiweiß, -e** egg white

der **Elektriker, –** electrician

Elektro– electrical

die **Eltern** (pl.) parents

empfehlen (empfiehlt), empfahl, empfohlen to recommend

das **Ende, -n** end; **kein Ende nehmen** to have no end

enden to end

das **Endrundenspiel, -e** playoff

eng narrow, cramped

England England

der **Engländer, –** Englishman

die **Engländerin, -nen** Englishwoman

entdecken to discover

die **Entfernung, -en** distance

enthalten (enthält), enthielt, enthalten to include, contain

entladen (entlädt), entlud, entladen to unload

sich **entscheiden, entschied sich, sich entschieden** to decide

entschuldigen to excuse

die **Entspannung** relaxation

entstehen, entstand, ist entstanden to arise

enttäuscht disappointed

die **Enttäuschung, -en** disappointment

entweichen, entwich, ist entwichen to escape, evade

entwickeln to develop

die **Entwicklung, -en** development

die **Erdbeere, -n** strawberry

die **Erde** earth

das **Erdgeschoß, -sse** ground floor

die **Erdkunde** geography

erfahren (erfährt), erfuhr, erfahren to learn, find out

die **Erfindung, -en** discovery

der **Erfolg, -e** success

erfolgen auf (+ acc.) to follow

erfolgreich successful

erforderlich required

die **Erfrischung, -en** refreshment

das **Ergebnis, -se** result

erhalten (erhält), erhielt, erhalten to receive, obtain

erkennen, erkannte, erkannt to recognize

sich **erkundigen** to inquire

erlangen to achieve, attain; **einen Beruf erlangen** to acquire a profession

erläutern to explain, illustrate

erleben to experience

das **Erlebnis, -se** experience; adventure

erledigen to take care of, execute

erleichtern to make easy, alleviate

ermöglichen to make possible

erneuern to renew, renovate

erreichen to reach

die **Erscheinung, -en** appearance

die **Ersparnisse** (pl.) savings

erstellen to make, set up

erstens first

erstklassig first–class

erwarten to expect

die **Erwartung, -en** expectancy

erwidern to reply; return; reciprocate

erwünscht desired

die **Erzählung, -en** story, narration

die **Erziehung** upbringing, education

der **Esprit** esprit

das **Essen, –** meal

die **Essenmünze, -n** coin purchased for meal in the university "Mensa."

der **Essig** vinegar

der **Eßtisch, -e** dining room table

das **Eßzimmer, –** dining room

die **Etage, -n** floor, story

der **Europäer, –** European

evangelisch Protestant

eventuell possibly

das **Examen, –** exam; **sich zum Examen melden** to apply to take an exam; **ein Examen bestehen, bestand, bestanden** to pass an exam; **in einem Examen durch·fallen (fällt durch), fiel durch, ist durchgefallen** to fail an exam

die **Existenz, -en** existence

exklusiv exclusive

explodieren to explode

das **Extrabett, -en** extra bed

das **Fach, ⸚er** subject

der **Facharbeiter, –** skilled worker, specialist

das **Fachbereich, -e** subject, discipline, specialization

die **Fachschule, -n** trade school

fahren (fährt), fuhr, ist gefahren to drive, ride, travel (by vehicle)

die **Fahrkarte, -n** ticket; **die einfache Fahrkarte, -n** one-way ticket

der **Fahrkartenschalter, –** ticket window

der **Fahrplan, ⸚e** timetable

das **Fahrrad, ⸚er** bicycle

der **Fahrstuhl, ⸚e** elevator

das **Fahrzeug, -e** motor vehicle

der **Fall, ⸚e** case; **auf keinen Fall** in no case

fallen (fällt), fiel, ist gefallen to fall

fällig due

falls in case

die **Familie, -n** family

die **Familienfeier, -n** family celebration

das **Familienmitglied, -er** family member

der **Familienstand** family status

der **Farbfernseher, –** color television

der **Farbfilm, –e** color film

das **Faß, ⸚er** barrel, keg

fast almost

faul lazy

faulenzen to be idle, laze around

das **Federbett, -en** feather bed

feiern to celebrate

das **Feld, -er** field; square

das **Fenster, –** window

die **Ferien** (*pl.*) vacation; **in die Ferien fahren** to take a vacation

der **Fernsehapparat, -e** television set

fern·sehen (sieht fern), sah fern, ferngesehen to watch television

das **Fernsehen** television; **im Fernsehen** on television

das **Fernsehgerät, -e** TV set

der **Fernsprecher, –** telephone

das **Fest, -e** festival, banquet

festlich festive

der **Festpreis, -e** firm price

fest·stellen to determine

das **Fett** fat, grease

feuern to fire

feuerrot fire engine red

die **Figur, -en** figure

die **Filmkamera, -s** movie camera

der **Filmstar, -s** film star

die **Filmvorstellung, -en** film showing

finden, fand, gefunden to find

Finnland Finland

finster dark

die **Firma, -men** firm

der **Fisch, -e** fish, Pisces (*astr.*)

der **Fischer, –** fisherman

der **Fitnessraum, ⸚e** fitness room, gym

das **Fleisch** meat

fließen, floß, ist geflossen to flow

flink quick; alert

der **Flirt, -s** flirtation

der **Flug, ⸚e** flight

der **Flughafen, ⸚** airport

der **Flur, -e** hall

der **Fluß, ⸚sse** river

fordern to demand

die **Forelle, -n** trout

formell formal

das **Formular, -e** form

die **Forstwissenschaft** forestry

das **Foto, -s** photograph

der **Fotoapparat, -e** camera

das **Fotogeschäft, -e** photo store

die **Fotografie, -n** photograph

fotografieren to photograph

das **Fotomodell, -e** model

die **Frage, -n** question; **eine Frage stellen** to ask a question

Frankreich France

der **Franzose, -n** Frenchman

die **Französin, -nen** Frenchwoman

französisch French

die **Frau, -en** woman; wife

die **Freizeit** free time

die **Fremdsprache, -n** foreign language

fressen (frißt) fraß, gefressen to eat (Refers to animals' eating. When applied to people, this expression has a vulgar connotation.)

die **Freude, -n** joy

sich **freuen** to be happy; **sich freuen über** (+ *acc.*) to be happy about

der **Freund, -e** friend, boyfriend

die **Freundschaft, -en** friendship

der **Friedhof, ⸚e** cemetery

frisch fresh

der **Friseur, -e** hairdresser

fröhlich happy, cheerful

der **Frost, ⸚e** frost

die **Frucht, ⸚e** fruit

früh early

der **Frühling** spring

das **Frühstück, -e** breakfast

frühstücken to have breakfast

sich **fühlen** to feel

führend leading

der **Führerschein, -e** driver's license

die **Führung, -en** tour

187

der **Fuß,** ⁼e foot; **zu Fuß** on foot; **zu Fuß gehen** to walk, go by foot

der **Fußball,** ⁼e football

der **Fußgänger,** – pedestrian

die **Fußgängerzone, -n** pedestrian zone, mall

G

die **Gabel, -n** fork

die **Gallone, -n** gallon

der **Gang,** ⁼e gear, hallway

ganz entire, whole

ganztags full days

die **Garage, -n** garage

die **Garantie, -n** guaranty, warranty

garantieren to guarantee, warrantee

die **Garderobe, -n** hall closet, part of foyer used to hang up clothes

die **Gardine, -n** curtain

der **Garten,** ⁼ garden, yard (front and back)

der **Gast,** ⁼e guest; customer (in restaurants and hotels)

der **Gastarbeiter,** – foreign worker

das **Gästezimmer,** – guest room

die **Gaststätte, -n** restaurant; inn

der **Gastwirt, -e** innkeeper

das **Gebäude,** – building

geben (gibt), gab, gegeben to give; **es gibt** there is, there are

das **Gebiet, -e** area

das **Gebirge,** – mountain range

geboren born

gebrauchen to use

gebraucht used

der **Gebrauchtwagen,** – used car

die **Gebrüder** (pl.) brothers

der **Geburtsort, -e** place of birth

das **Gebüsch, -e** shrubbery

das **Gedächtnis, -se** memory

die **Geduld** patience

geeignet suitable

die **Gefahr, -en** danger

gefallen (gefällt), gefiel, gefallen (+ dat.) to please

das **Gefängnis, -se** jail

der **Gefrierpunkt** freezing point

das **Gefühl, -e** feeling

der **Gegensatz,** ⁼e contradiction, opposite

der **Gegenstand,** ⁼e object

das **Gehalt,** ⁼er salary

gehen, ging, ist gegangen to go, walk; **gehen um** to have to do with

gehören (zu) to belong (to)

die **Geisteswissenschaften** humanities

gekleidet dressed

gelangen to reach, arrive at, attain to

das **Geld, -er** money; **Geld bei sich haben** to have money with you

der **Geldwechsel,** – money exchange

gelegentlich occasionally

gelten (gilt), galt, gegolten to be valid

gemeinsam mutual, together; **miteinander gemeinsam haben** to have in common

die **Gemeinschaft, -en** community

die **Gemeinschaftskunde** social studies

das **Gemüse,** – vegetable

gemütlich comfortable

genau exact, precise

genießen, genoß, genossen to enjoy

geöffnet open

die **Geographie** geography

das **Gepäck** luggage

der **Gepäckwagen,** – baggage car

gepflegt well–groomed

gerade, straight; **gerade angekommen** just arrived

das **Gerät, -e** equipment

geräumig roomy, spacious

das **Gericht, -e** dish, course; court of justice

die **Germanistik** German studies

das **Geschäft, -e** store

geschehen (geschieht), geschah, ist geschehen to happen

das **Geschenk, -e** present, gift

die **Geschichte, -n** story, account; history

geschickt skillful, adroit

geschieden divorced

das **Geschirr** dishes

die **Geschirrspülmaschine,-n** dishwasher

geschlossen closed

das **Geschoß, -sse** floor, story (cannot be used for floors higher than the second, the **Obergeshoß**)

die **Geschwister** (pl.) brothers and sisters

die **Geselligkeit** social life

das **Gesetz, -e** law

das **Gespräch, -e** conversation

der **Gesprächsstoff,** -e conversational material

gesund healthy

die **Gesundheit** health

geteilt divided

getönt tinted

das **Getränk, -e** drink

das **Getriebe,** – transmission

gewinnen, gewann, gewonnen to win

das **Gewitter,** – thunderstorm

gewöhnt accustomed; **an etwas** (acc.) **gewöhnt sein** to be accustomed to something

das **Gewürz, -e** spice, seasoning
das **Gipsbein, -e** plaster leg cast
das **Glas, ̈er** glass
glauben (+ *dat. with people*) to be-lieve
gleich similar, immediately
die **Gleichung, -en** equation
das **Gleis, -e** track
der **Globus, -se** globe
das **Glück** happiness, luck
der **Glühwein** hot spiced wine
GmbH (= Gesellschaft mit be-schränkter Haftung) company (with limited liability)
das **Gramm** gram (100 g. = 3.5 ounces)
greifen, griff, gegriffen to seize; **greifen nach** to reach for
die **Grenze, -n** border; **an der Grenze** at the border
grenzen an (+ *acc.*) to border on
Griechenland Greece
griechisch Greek
grillen to barbecue, grill
die **Größe, -n** size
der **Großhandel** wholesale
die **Großmutter, ̈** grandmother
großräumig spacious
der **Großvater, ̈** grandfather
großzügig generous
der **Grund, ̈e** reason
gründen to establish, found
die **Grundlage, -n** basis
die **Gruppe, -n** group
grüßen to greet
die **Gunst** favor, good will
günstig reasonable, favorable: **günstig gelegen** to be favorably situated or located
die **Gurke, -n** cucumber, pickle
der **Gürtel, –** belt
gutaussehend good looking
der **Güterzug, ̈e** freight train
gütig kind, benevolent
das **Gymnasium, -ien** secondary school (attended from ages 10–19)

H

die **Hacke, -n** hoe
die **Haft** arrest, imprisonment
halbtags half days
halten (hält), hielt, gehalten to hold; **halten von** to think of
die **Haltestelle, -n** bus stop, tram stop
der **Hamburger, –** hamburger
der **Hammer, –** hammer
die **Hand, ̈e** hand; **anhand von** by means of

die **Handarbeit** needlework
die **Handdusche, -n** hand shower
der **Handel** commerce
handeln to trade, bargain; **handeln von** to be about
handgeschrieben handwritten
der **Händler, –** dealer
das **Handrührgerät, -e** mixer
der **Handschuh, -e** glove
das **Handtuch, ̈er** towel
der **Handwahrsager, –** palmist (*masc.*)
die **Handwahrsagerin, -nen** palmist (*fem.*)
der **Handwerker, –** artisan, craftsman
hängen an (+ *acc.*) to attach to
der **Hauptbahnhof, ̈e** main railway station
das **Hauptfach, ̈er** major (subject)
die **Hauptschule, -n** school attended from ages 6–10 or 6–15
die **Hauptstadt, ̈e** capitol
die **Hausangestellte, -n** house employee (*fem.*)
der **Häuserblock, ̈e** block of houses
hausgemacht homemade
der **Haushalt, -e** household
das **Haushaltsgerät, -e** household appliance
die **Haushaltswaren** (*pl.*) household articles
häuslich domestic
das **Hausmädchen, –** maid
der **Hausmeister, –** caretaker, janitor
der **Hausschlüssel, –** front door key
der **Hauswirt, -e** landlord
die **Heckscheibe, -n** rear window
der **Heckspoiler, –** rear spoiler
das **Heft, -e** notebook
die **Heimatstadt, ̈e** native city
die **Heiratsanzeige, -n** marriage advertisement
heiß hot
heißen, heiß, geheißen to be called
heiter clear, bright
die **Heizung, -en** heater, heating
der **Helm, -e** helmet
das **Hemd, -en** shirt
die **Herausforderung, -en** challenge
der **Herbst, -e** fall, autumn
der **Herd, -e** stove, range
die **Herdplatte, -n** burner
die **Herrenbekleidung** men's clothing
die **Herrenboutique, -en** men's boutique
das **Herrengeschäft, -e** men's store
herrschen to reign, rule
herzensgut kindhearted
der **Herzenskummer** sadness of the heart
herzlich affectionate, warm

heute today

heutzutage these days

die Hilfe help

sich hinein·versetzen to project oneself into

hin·fallen (fällt hin), fiel hin, ist hingefallen to fall down

der Hinflug, ⸚e one-way flight (to a destination)

die Hinrichtung, -en execution

der Hintergrund, ⸚e background

hinterher afterwards

das Hobby, -s hobby

das Hochdruckgebiet, -e high pressure area

die Hochschule, -n college, university

die Höchsttemperatur, -en highest temperature

der Hof, ⸚e yard, courtyard; farm

das Hofbräuhaus beer hall in Munich

hoffentlich it is to be hoped

die Höhe, -n amount; height, summit

der Honig honey

hören to hear

das Horoskop, -e horoscope; jemandem das Horoskop stellen to tell someone's horoscope

der Hörsaal, -säle lecture hall

die Hose, -n trousers

das Hotel, -s hotel

hübsch pretty, cute

hungrig hungry

der Hurrikan, -e hurricane

der Hut, ⸚e hat

I

ideal ideal

die Illustrierte, -n, -n illustrated magazine

die Imbißstube, -n snack bar

die Information, -en information; Informationen aus·geben (gibt aus), gab aus, ausgegeben to provide information

sich informieren to inform oneself

der Inhalt content(s)

inklusive inclusive

der Inklusivpreis, -e inclusive price

das Inland inland, domestic

innen inside

das Innere interior

die Insel, -n island

das Inserat, -e advertisement

die Instandhaltung maintenance, upkeep

das Interesse, -n interest

sich interessieren für to have an interest in

irgendwas something

Irland Ireland

Italien Italy

der Italiener, – Italian (masc.)

die Italienerin, -nen Italian (fem.)

italienisch Italian

J

die Jacke, -n jacket, sport jacket

jagen to hunt

der Jäger, – hunter

die Jahreszeit, -en season

das Jahrhundert, -e century

die Jeans (pl.) jeans

jeweils respectively

der Job, -s job

der Joghurt yogurt

jüdisch Jewish

jugendlich youthful

der Jugendliche, -n, -n young person from 14 to 18

(das) Jugoslawien Yugoslavia

der Junge, -n, -n boy, young man

der Junggeselle, -n bachelor

K

das Kabriolett, -e convertible

der Käfer, – bug

der Kaffee coffee

der Kaffeeautomat,-en coffeemaker

das Kakaogetränk, -e chocolate drink

der Kalender, – calendar

kalkulieren to calculate

die Kalorie, -n calorie

die Kaltfront, -en cold front

die Kamera, -s camera

der Kamin, -e fireplace

sich kämmen to comb one's hair

der Kanal, ⸚e channel

der Kanzler, – chancellor

die Kartei, -en card catalog

der Kartoffelsalat potato salad

die Käseplatte, -n cheese platter

die Kasse, -n cashier's desk, cash register, check-out counter

die Kassiererin, -nen cashier, checker (fem.)

das Kästchen, – small chest

der Kastenwagen, – van

der Kater, – tom cat; hangover

das Katergefühl, -e hungover feeling

die Kathedrale, -n cathedral

katholisch catholic

der Kauf, ⸚e purchase, bargain

190

kaufen to buy

der **Käufer, –** buyer

das **Kaufhaus, ⸚er** department store

kaum scarcely

der **Keller, –** cellar

der **Kellner, –** waiter

die **Kellnerin, -nen** waitress

kennen·lernen to become acquainted with; get to know

das **Kennzeichen, –** sign, distinguishing mark

kennzeichnen to mark, designate

die **Kerze, -n** candle

das **Kilo (gramm)** kilogram (= 2.2 lbs.)

der **Kilometer, –** kilometer (= 0.6 miles)

der **Kindergarten, ⸚** kindergarten

kinderlieb fond of children

das **Kino, -s** movie theater

der **Kinogänger, –** movie–goer

der **Kiosk, -e** newsstand

die **Kirche, -n** church

die **Kirsche, -n** cherry

das **Kissen, –** pillow

der **Kittel, –** smock

klar clear

die **Klasse, -n** class; **erster Klasse fahren** to travel first class; **zweiter Klasse fahren** to travel second class

der **Klassenkamerad, -en, -en** classmate

das **Kleid, -er** dress

der **Kleiderschrank, ⸚e** wardrobe

die **Kleidung** clothes, clothing

der **Kleinlaster, –** pick-up truck

das **Klima, -ta** climate

die **Klimaanlage, -n** air conditioning

klingen to sound

klirr! smash!

der **Knödel, –** dumpling

kochen to cook

die **Kochkenntnisse** (pl.) cooking knowledge

der **Koffer, –** suitcase

der **Kofferkuli, -s** luggage cart

der **Kofferraum, ⸚e** trunk (auto)

der **Kollege, -n, -n** colleague (masc.)

der **Kollegenkreis, -e** circle of colleagues; faculty

die **Kollegin, -nen** colleague (fem.)

der **Kombiwagen, –** station wagon

der **Komfort** luxury

der **Kommilitone, -n, -n** fellow–student (masc.)

die **Kommilitonin, -nen** fellow–student (fem.)

der **Konditor, -en** pastry–baker

die **Konditorei, -en** café–bakery

konfessionslos no religious affiliation

der **König, -e** king

die **Königin, -nen** queen

der **Kontakt, -e** contact; **Kontakte an·knüpfen** to make contacts

die **Kontaktlinse, -n** contact lens

der **Kopf, ⸚e** head

die **Kopfschmerzen** (pl.) headache; **Kopfschmerzen bereiten** to cause a headache

der **Kopierer, –** copier

der **Korb, ⸚e** basket

die **Körpergröße, -n** height

körperlich physical

die **Körpertemperatur** body temperature

korpulent corpulent, fat

die **Kost** food, board

kosten to cost

kostenlos without cost

das **Kraftfahrzeug (KFZ), -e** motor vehicle

kräftig strong

die **Krankenschwester, -n** nurse

die **Krawatte, -n** tie

der **Kredit, -e** credit

die **Kreditkarte, -n** credit card

die **Kreide** chalk

kreisen to circle

die **Kreuzung, -en** crossing

der **Krimi, -s** detective story

kritisch critical

der **Kronleuchter, –** chandelier

der **Krug, ⸚e** mug, pitcher

die **Küche, -n** kitchen

der **Kuchen, –** cake

der **Kugelschreiber, –** ball point pen

der **Kühlschrank, ⸚e** refrigerator

der **Kunde, -n, -n** customer (masc.)

der **Kundendienst** customer service

die **Kundin, -nen** customer (fem.)

die **Kunst, ⸚e** art

die **Kunsterziehung** art education

die **Kupplung, -en** clutch

der **Kurs, -e** course, exchange rate; **einen Kurs belegen** to take a course

der **Kurswagen, –** passenger car of a train which is destined for a certain city

kurz short; **seit kurzem** since recently

kürzlich a short time ago

das **Küstengebiet, -e** coastal area

191

L ———————————————————

lächeln to smile

der **Laden, ⸚** shop

der **Ladenbesitzer, –** shop owner

der **Ladenchef, -s** shop manager

der **Ladendieb, -e** shoplifter

der **Ladendiebstahl** shoplifting
der **Ladentisch, -e** counter
die **Lage, -n** situation; **in der Lage sein** to be capable, to be in a position
die **Lampe, -n** lamp
das **Land, ̈er** country
die **Landkarte, -n** map
der **Landwirt, -e** farmer
die **Landwirtschaft** agriculture
lang long
lassen (läßt), ließ, gelassen to leave, let
das **Leben, –** life
der **Lebenslauf, ̈e** resumé
die **Lebensmittel** (pl.) groceries
das **Lebensmittelgeschäft, -e** grocery store
der **Lebensstandard, -s** living standard
auf Lebenszeit for life
der **Leberkäs** liver loaf
der **Ledersitz, -e** leather seat
die **Ledertasche, -n** leather pocketbook
die **Lederwaren** (pl.) leather goods
das **Lederwarengeschäft, -e** leather goods store
ledig single
leer empty
leeren to empty
die **Leerung, -en** (mail) collection
der **Lehm** mud, clay
die **Lehre, -n** apprenticeship, teaching
der **Lehrer, –** teacher (masc.)
die **Lehrerin, -nen** teacher (fem.)
leicht easy
leider unfortunately
die **Leistung, -en** performance, accomplishment
der **Leiter, –** leader
die **Leiter, -n** ladder
die **Lektüre, -n** readings, reading matter
die **Lenkhilfe** power steering
lernen to study (lessons); learn
das **Lesepult, -e** lecturn
die **Leute** (pl.) people
das **Licht, -er** light
das **Lichtbild, -er** photograph
lieb dear
die **Liebe** love
liebenswert dear, worthy of love
das **Liebhaben** fondness, love
das **Liebhaberstück, -e** collector's item
Lieblings– favorite
die **Lieblingsstadt, ̈e** favorite city
liegen, lag, gelegen to lie; **liegen an** (+ dat.) to be situated at
der **Liegewagen,** couchette, sleeping car (less luxurious than a **Schlafwagen**)
die **Limo, -s** lemon soda

die **Limousine, -n** sedan
links left
der **Liter, –** liter (= 1.06 quarts)
die **Literaturwissenschaft** literary criticism
der **Löffel, –** spoon
sich **lohnen** to be worthwhile
das **Lokal, -e** tavern
die **Lokomotive, -n** engine
lösen to solve; dissolve
die **Lösung, -en** solution
die **Luft, ̈e** air
die **Luftbewegung, -en** air movement
der **Luftdruck** air pressure
die **Luftpost** air mail; **per Luftpost** by airmail
der **Lümmel, –** lout, ruffian, boor

M

machen to do, make; **das Abitur machen** to pass the qualifying examination; **sich über jemanden lustig machen** to make fun of someone
das **Mädchen, –** girl
der **Magen, ̈** stomach
die **Mahlzeit, -en** meal, mealtime
das **Mal, -e** time, point in time; **zum ersten Mal** for the first time
der **Maler, –** painter
manchmal sometimes
die **Mandel, -n** almond; tonsil
mangelhaft deficient
mangeln to lack
der **Mann, ̈er** husband; man
männlich male
der **Mantel, ̈** coat
das **Märchen, –** fairy tale
die **Margarine** margarine
der **Markt, ̈e** market
der **Marktplatz, ̈e** market place
die **Marmelade, -n** jam
die **Maß, –** liter of beer
die **Massage, -n** massage
massenweise en masse, in large numbers
die **Maßnahme, -n** measure, precaution
die **Mathematik** mathematics
die **Mauer, -n** wall
der **Maurer, –** mason
der **Mechaniker, –** mechanic
mechanisch mechanical
die **Medizin** medicine
das **Meer, -e** sea
das **Mehl** flour
die **Mehrwertsteuer, -n (MWSt.)** German sales tax

die **Meile, -n** mile
die **Meinung, -en** opinion
meistens mostly
die **Menge, -n** quantity, a great deal
der **Mensch, -en, -en** person, human being
menschlich human
merken to notice
sich **merken** to remember
die **Meßdaten** (pl.) measurement data
messen (mißt), maß, gemessen to measure
das **Messer, –** knife
der **Meteorologe, -n, -n** meteorologist
der **Metzger, –** butcher
die **Miederwaren** (pl.) foundation garments
mieten to rent
die **Milch** milk
minderjährig juvenile
mindestens at least
die **Minute, -n** minute
mischen to mix
mit·bringen, brachte mit, mitgebracht to bring along
mit·denken, dachte mit, mitgedacht to think along with
das **Mitglied, -er** member
mit·nehmen (nimmt mit), nahm mit, mitgenommen to take along
das **Mittagessen, –** lunch; **zu Mittag essen** to eat lunch
die **Mittagszeit, -en** noontime
mittelmäßig mediocre
die **„Mittlere Reife"** diploma from a German "Realschule"
mit·zahlen to share expenses
die **Möbel** (pl.) furniture
das **Möbelstück, -e** piece of furniture
die **Mode, -n** fashion
modern modern
die **Modewaren** (pl.) fashions
modisch fashionable
die **Möglichkeit, -en** possibility
mollig pleasingly plump
der **Moment, -e** moment, instant; **in dem Moment** at the moment
die **Monarchie, -n** monarchy
monatlich monthly
das **Monatsgehalt, ¨er** monthly salary
die **Moral** moral, morals
der **Motor, -en** engine
das **Motorrad, ¨er** motorcycle
der **Motorschaden, ¨** blown engine
die **Musiksendung, -en** musical program
musizieren to play music
die **Mutter, ¨** mother
die **Mütze, -n** cap

N _____

das **Nachbarland, ¨er** bordering country
nach·erzählen to retell, recite
nachmittags afternoons
die **Nachspeise, -n** dessert
nächst next
der **Nachteil, -e** disadvantage
die **Nachthaube, -n** sleeping bonnet
der **Nachtisch, -e** dessert
der **Nachtportier, -s** night porter
nachts at night
der **Nachttisch, -e** night table
der **Nagellack, -e** nail polish
nah near
die **Nähe** nearness, proximity; **in der Nähe von** close to, in the vicinity of; **in nächster Nähe** very nearby
die **Nähmaschine, -n** sewing machine
naiv naive
der **Name, -ns, -n** name
nämlich namely
die **Naturwissenschaften** (pl.) natural science
der **Nebel** fog
der **Nebelscheinwerfer, –** fog light
die **Nebenarbeit, -en** extra work
das **Nebenfach, ¨er** minor (subject or course)
der **Neffe, -n, -n** nephew
nennen, nannte, genannt to name
nett nice
neugierig curious
nicht–rauchend non–smoking
der **Nichtraucher, –** non–smoker
nie never
die **Niederlande** Netherlands
niedrig low
das **Niveau, -s** plane, level; class
der **Norden** north
nördlich north, northern, northerly
Norwegen Norway
der **Norweger, –** Norwegian (masc.)
die **Norwegerin, -nen** Norwegian (fem.)
norwegisch Norwegian
die **Note, -n** grade
nötig necessary
die **Notizen** (pl.) notes; **sich Notizen machen** (acc.) to take notes
nüchtern sober
das **Nummernschild, -er** license plate
nützlich useful

O _____

der **Ober, –** waiter
die **Oberbekleidung** outerwear

das **Obergeschoß, -sse** second story (**Geschoß** cannot be used for floors higher than the second.)

das **Oberhemd, -en** dress shirt

das **Obst, –sorten** fruit

der **Ofen, ⸗** oven

die **Öffnungszeiten** (*pl.*) store hours

der **Ohrring, -e** earring

das **Öl, -e** oil

der **Ölwechsel, –** oil change

das **Olympiabad** Olympic pool (Munich)

der **Omnibus, -se** bus

der **Onkel, –** uncle

die **Oper, -n** opera

der **Opernbesuch, -e** opera attendance

optisch optically

das **Orangen–Kaltgetränk, -e** orangeade

der **Orangensaft** orange juice

ordentlich tidy

die **Ordung, -en** order; **in Ordnung** in order

der **Osten** east, East

Österreich Austria

der **Österreicher, –** Austrian (*masc.*)

die **Österreicherin, -nen** Austrian (*fem.*)

östlich east, easterly, eastern

der **Ozean, -e** ocean

P _____

das **Paar, -e** pair; **ein paar** a few, several

das **Paket, -e** package, parcel

der **Palast, ⸗e** palace

die **Panne, -n** breakdown (automobile), flat tire

das **Papier, -e** paper

die **Parfümerie, -n** cosmetics department

parken to park

der **Parkplatz, ⸗e** parking place

die **Parkuhr, -en** parking meter

der **Partner, –** partner (*masc.*)

die **Partnerin, -nen** partner (*fem.*)

die **Party, -ies** party

der **Paß, ⸗e** passport; **den Pass vorzeigen** to show one's passport

passen to fit; **passen zu** to be suitable for

passieren, ist passiert to happen, occur

die **Pause, -n** pause, break

der **Pelz, -e** fur

der **Pelzmantel, ⸗** fur coat

der **Pensionspreis, -e** pension, boarding house price

perfekt perfect

die **Person, -en** person

die **Personalabteilung, -en** personnel department

der **Personalchef, -s** personnel manager

der **Pfeffer, –** pepper

die **Pfeife, -n** pipe

der **Pfennig, -e** pfennig, penny

der **Pfirsich, -e** peach

die **Pflanze, -n** plant

pflegen to take care of

die **Pflicht, -en** duty

das **Pflichtfach, ⸗er** required course

die **Phantasie, -n** fantasy

die **Physik** physics

das **Picknick, -s** picnic

die **Pistole, -n** pistol, gun

die **Pizza, -s** pizza

der **PKW (Personenkraftwagen), –** passenger car

das **Plakat, -e** poster

der **Plan, ⸗e** plan

planen to plan

die **Planung** planning

der **Platz, ⸗e** place, square

plötzlich suddenly

Polen Poland

polieren to polish

die **Politesse, -n** meter maid

die **Politik** politics

der **Polizist, -en, -en** policeman

die **Pommes frites** french fries

der **Portier, -s** porter

die **Portion, -en** portion

Portugal Portugal

das **Porzellan** china, porcelain

die **Post (-en)** post office, mail; **auf die Post gehen** to go to the post office; **auf der Post** at the post office

das **Postamt, ⸗er** post office; **auf dem Postamt** at the post office

das **Postfach, ⸗er** P.O. box

die **Postgebühr, -en** postal fee

die **Postkarte, -n** postcard

die **Postleitzahl, -en** zip code

der **Poststempel, –** postmark

praktisch practical

der **Preis, -e** price; **Preise inklusive gesetzliche Mehrwertsteuer (MWSt.)** Prices include legal sales tax

preiswert reasonable, worth the money

der **Privatbesitzer, –** private owner

die **Privatsache, -n** private matter

probieren to test, try, taste

das **Problem, -e** problem

problematisch problematic

der **Problemfilm, -e** movie with artistic merit

das **Produkt, -e** product

der **Professor, -en** professor

der **Profi, -s** professional

das **Profil, -e** profile

194

das **Programm, -e** program, channel
der **Programmierer, –** programmer *(masc.)*
die **Programmiererin, -nen** programmer *(fem.)*
das **Proseminar, -e** proseminar (lecture–discussion usually with paper required)
Pros(i)t Cheers! toast (to someone's health)
der **Prospekt, -e** prospectus, pamphlet
prüfen to test
die **Prüfung, -en** test, exam; **eine Prüfung machen** to take a test (see **Examen** for other usages)
die **Psyche** psyche
die **Psychologie** psychology
die **Publikation, -en** publication
der **Pulli, -s** sweater, pullover
der **Pullover, –** sweater, pullover
pünktlich punctual, on time
die **Puppe, -n** doll
das **Putzmittel, –** scouring detergent

Q

qualifiziert qualified
die **Qualität, -en** quality

R

rad·fahren (fährt Rad) fuhr Rad, ist radgefahren to ride a bicycle
das **Radio, -s** radio; **im Radio** on the radio
der **Rat, -schläge** advice; **einen guten Rat geben** to give a good piece of advice; **um Rat fragen** to ask for advice
die **Rate, -n** installment payment; **auf Raten kaufen** to buy on installments
raten to guess
die **Ratenzahlung, -en** installment payment
der **Ratenzahlungsvertrag, ̈e** installment payment contract
der **Ratschlag, ̈e** piece of advice, suggestion
der **Rauch** smoke
rauchen to smoke
der **Raucher** smoker; smoking car of a train
der **Raum, ̈e** room; **im Raum** in the area
reagieren auf (+ *acc.*) to react to
die **Realschule, -n** school attended from ages 10–16
der **Rechen, –** rake
die **Rechenmaschine, -n** calculator
rechnen to figure; calculate

die **Rechnung, -en** bill, check
das **Recht, -e** right; law
recht correct, just, very; **recht haben** to be correct; **recht tun** (+ *dat.*) to please
rechts right
der **Rechtsanwalt, ̈e** attorney
rechtzeitig prompt
reden to speak
reduziert reduced
das **Referat, -e** oral and written paper
der **Regen** rain
der **Regenfall, ̈e** rainfall, precipitation
die **Regierung, -en** government
die **Regierungsform, -en** form of government
die **Registrierkasse, -n** cash register
regnen to rain
die **Reiberei, -en** conflict
reif mature
der **Reifen, –** tire
die **Reifenpanne, -n** flat tire
die **Reinigung, -en** cleaners, laundry
die **Reise, -n** trip; **eine Reise machen** to take a trip
das **Reisebüro, -s** travel agency
der **Reiseführer, –** tour guide
reiselustig fond of travelling
reisen, ist gereist to travel
der **Reiseproviant** travel provisions
das **Reiten** horseback riding
reizen to excite, stimulate
das **Rendezvous, –** rendezvous
der **Rennfahrer, –** race car driver
der **Rentner, –** pensioner
die **Reparatur, -en** repair
reparieren to repair
repräsentativ distinguished
der **Rest, -e** rest
das **Restaurant, -s** restaurant
die **Restbestände** (*pl.*) remnants
restlich remaining
das **Rezept, -e** recipe; prescription
richten an (+ *acc.*) to direct to
der **Richter, –** judge
richtig right, correct
das **Richtige** the right thing
die **Richtung, -en** direction
die **Rindsbratwurst, ̈e** (beef) bratwurst
die **Rolle, -n** rôle; **eine Rolle spielen** to play a rôle, be a factor
die **Rolltreppe, -n** escalator
der **Roman, -e** novel
rostfrei rust–free
der **Rücken, –** back
die **Rückfahrkarte, -n** round–trip ticket
die **Rückkehr** return
der **Rucksack, ̈e** back pack
die **Ruhe** rest

die **Ruhezone, -n** rest area
das **Rührei, -er** scrambled eggs
der **Ruin** ruin, downfall
Rumänien Rumania
der **Rundfunk** radio
der **Russe, -n** Russian *(masc.)*
die **Russin, -nen** Russian *(fem.)*
russisch Russian
Rußland Russia
rüstig hale and hearty

S

das **Sachbuch, ̈er** non–fiction
die **Sache, -n** thing, article
der **Sack, ̈e** bag
die **Sahne** cream
der **Sakko, -s** sport jacket
der **Salat, -e salad**
salopp relaxed; informal
das **Salz** salt
die **Salzkartoffeln** *(pl.)* boiled potatoes
sammeln to gather
samstags Saturdays
das **Sandwich, -es** sandwich
der **Sänger, –** singer *(masc.)*
die **Sängerin, -nen** singer *(fem.)*
der **Satellit, -en** satellite
satt satisfied, full
die **Sauce, -n** sauce
der **Sauerbraten, –** roast beef
die **Sauna, -s** sauna
die **S–Bahn (Stadtbahn), -en** subway that travels also above ground outside the city
das **Schachbrett, -er** chess board
der **Schadenersatz** damages, compensation
schaffen, schuf, geschaffen to create
der **Schaffner, –** conductor
die **Schale, -n** peel, skin
die **Schallplatte, -n** record album
schalten to shift
der **Schalter, –** counter window
der **Schalterbeamte, -n, -n** ticket agent
schamlos shameless
scharf sharp; **scharf rechnen** to calculate carefully
der **Schauer, –** showers
der **Schein, -e** bill (money note)
scheinen to seem, appear
der **Scheinwerfer, –** headlight
schenken to present, give
die **Schere, -n** scissors
das **Schiebedach, ̈er** sun roof
schieben, schob, geschoben to push
schießen, schoß, geschossen to shoot

der **Schiffsoffizer, -e** ship's officer
das **Schild, -er** sign; **auf dem Schild stehen** to be on the sign
schildern to describe, portray
der **Schilling, -e** shilling
der **Schinken, –** ham
der **Schirm, -e** umbrella
schlafen (schläft), schlief, geschlafen to sleep
der **Schlafsack, ̈e** sleeping bag
der **Schlafwagen, –** sleeping car
der **Schlag** whipped cream
schlagen (schlägt), schlug, geschlagen to beat, whip
das **Schlagwort, -e** slogan
schlampig sloppy, untidy
die **Schlange, -n** snake; line
schlank slender, slim
schlecht bad, poor, inferior; **Mir ist schlecht.** I feel ill.
schleppen to pull, drag
schließen, schloß, geschlossen to close; conclude
das **Schließfach, ̈er** locker
schlimm bad
der **Schlips, -e** tie
der **Schluß, ̈e** end, finish, conclusion; **Schluß machen** to terminate
der **Schlüssel, –** key
der **Schlußverkauf, ̈e** final bargain sale (in winter and summer in Germany)
schmecken to taste
der **Schmied, -e** blacksmith
der **Schmuck** jewelry
das **Schmuckwarengeschäft, -e** jewelry store
das **Schmusen** kissing, necking
der **Schnee** snow
schneiden, schnitt, geschnitten to cut
der **Schneider, –** tailor
schnell fast, quick
die **Schnellwäsche** express laundry
der **Schnellzug, ̈e** express train
die **Schokolade** (hot) chocolate
schonen to treat with consideration, take good care of
der **Schornstein, -e** chimney
der **Schrank, ̈e** closet
schreiben, schrieb, geschrieben to write; **schreiben an** (+ *acc.*) to write to
die **Schreibmaschine, -n** typewriter
der **Schreibtisch, -e** desk
die **Schreibwaren** *(pl.)* stationery
schreien, schrie, geschrien to cry, scream
die **Schrift, -en** writing, handwriting

schriftlich in writing
der **Schriftsteller, −** writer
die **Schublade, -n** drawer
der **Schuh, -e** shoe
das **Schuhgeschäft, -e** shoe store
die **Schulbildung** education
schuldig guilty
der **Schuldirektor, -en** school principal, superintendent
schuldlos guiltless
die **Schule, -n** school
der **Schüler, −** pupil *(masc.)*
die **Schülerin, -nen** pupil *(fem.)*
das **Schuljahr, -e** school year
die **Schürze, -n** apron
die **Schüssel, -n** bowl
der **Schuster, −** shoemaker
schütteln to shake
schützen to protect; **schützen vor** *(+ dat.)* to protect from
schwach weak, mild
die **Schwalbe, -n** swallow
schwänzen to cut class
das **Schwarzbrot** brown bread
schwarz·fahren, fuhr schwarz, ist schwarzgefahren to ride (tram, bus, subway) illegally without paying
der **Schwede, -n** Swede *(masc.)*
Schweden Sweden
die **Schwedin, -nen** Swede *(fem.)*
schwedisch Swedish
das **Schweigen** silence
das **Schweinefleisch** pork
die **Schweiz** Switzerland
der **Schweizer, −** Swiss native *(masc.)*
die **Schweizerin, -nen** Swiss native *(fem.)*
schwer difficult; heavy
die **Schwester, -n** sister
die **Schwierigkeit, -en** difficulty
das **Schwimmbad, ¨er** swimming pool
der **See, -n** lake
die **See** sea, ocean
die **Segeljacht, -en** sailing yacht
das **Segeln** sailing
sehbehindert visually impaired
die **Sekretärin, -nen** secretary *(fem.)*
selber self, myself, yourself, himself, etc.
selbst self, myself, yourself, himself, etc.; even
selbständig independent(ly)
der **Selbständige, -n** self−employed person
die **Selbstbedienung** self−service
selbstbewußt self−confident
selig blissful
selten seldom
das **Semester, −** semester

das **Seminar, -e** seminar
die **Semmel, -n** small hard roll
seriös serious
der **Service** table service
servieren to serve
die **Serviette, -n** napkin
die **Servolenkung** power steering
der **Sessel, −** armchair
sicher safe, secure; **sicher sein** to be certain
der **Sicherheitsgurt, -e** safety belt
der **Siedepunkt, -e** boiling point
silber−metallic metallic silver
der **Sinn** sense
der **Sitz, -e** seat
sitzen, saß, gesessen to sit
das **Skifahren** skiing
ski·laufen (läuft ski), lief ski, ist skigelaufen to ski; **skilaufen gehen** to go skiing
der **Skiträger, −** ski rack
das **Sofa, -s** sofa
sofort immediately
sogar even
der **Sohn, ¨e** son
solide reliable
der **Sommer, −** summer
die **Sommersprossen** *(pl.)* freckles
die **Sonnenterrasse, -n** sun terrace
sonnig sunny
sorgen für to take care of
die **Soßenschüssel, -n** gravy dish
die **Sozialwissenschaften** *(pl.)* social sciences
die **Soziologie** sociology
Spanien Spain
der **Spanier, −** Spaniard
die **Spanierin, -nen** Spanish woman
spanisch Spanish
sparsam thrifty
die **Sparsamkeit** thriftiness
der **Spaß, ¨e** joke, fun; **zum Spaß** for fun
spazieren·fahren (fährt spazieren), fuhr spazieren, ist spazierengefahren to drive around
die **Speise, -n** food
die **Speisekarte, -n** menu
der **Spiegel, −** mirror
die **Spiegeleier** *(pl.)* fried eggs
spielen to play
die **Spielwaren** *(pl.)* toys
das **Spielwarengeschäft, -e** toy store
spitz(ig) sharp, pointed
spontan spontaneously
der **Sport, -arten** sports; **Sport treiben, trieb, getrieben** to play sports
sportlich sporty, athletic

197

die **Sportsachen** *(pl.)* sporting goods
die **Sportveranstaltung, -en** sports event
der **Sportwagen, –** sports car
die **Sprachkenntnisse** *(pl.)* knowledge of a language
die **Sprachübung, -en** language practice and exercises
die **Sprachwissenschaft** linguistics
sprechen (spricht), sprach, gesprochen to speak
das **Sprechfunkgerät, -e** walkie–talkie
die **Springform, -en** spring-form pan
sprudeln to bubble, effervesce
der **Sprühregen** drizzle
spülen to wash dishes, rinse
die **Staatsangehörigkeit, -en** citizenship
das **Staatsexamen, -ina** state exam (final qualifying examination before graduation for German university students); diploma from a university
der **Stadtbummel, –** stroll through the city; **einen Stadtbummel machen** to take a stroll through the city
die **Stadtführung, -en** city tour
der **Stadtplan, ⁻e** city map
das **Stadtzentrum, -tren** center city
der **Stahlgürtelreifen, –** steel belted radial tire
der **Stamm, ⁻e** stem
stammen aus to come from, originate
der **Stand, ⁻e** stand
ständig economical
der **Standort, -e** site, location
die **Stange, -n** pole
stark strong
die **Statistik** statistics
statt·finden, fand statt, stattgefunden to take place
stattlich portly
das **Steak, -s** steak
die **Steckdose, -n** electrical outlet
stehen, stand, gestanden to stand
stehen·bleiben, blieb stehen, ist stehengeblieben to stop
die **Stehlampe, -n** floor lamp
steif stiff
steigern to increase
das **Stellenangebot, -e** job advertisement
die **Stellung, -en** job
die **Stereoanlage, -n** stereo system
das **Stereo–Kassetten–Radio, -s** stereo-cassette radio
das **Sternzeichen, –** sign *(astr.)*
die **Steuer, -n** tax
die **Stiftsbibliothek, -en** monastery library
stimmen to be correct, to be all right; **das stimmt** that's right
das **Stockwerk, -e** story, floor

der **Stoff, -e** fabric
das **Stopplicht, -er** brake light
der **Stoßdämpfer, –** shock absorber
stoßen (stößt), stieß, gestoßen to push, shove
die **Stoßstange, -n** bumper
die **Strafanzeige, -n** summons; **eine Strafanzeige erstatten gegen jemanden** to make a report to police against someone regarding a punishable offense
die **Strafe, -n** penalty, fine
die **Straftat, -en** punishable offense
der **Strafzettel, –** ticket, summons
die **Straße, -n** street; **auf der Straße** on the street; **in der Leopold Straße** on Leopold Street
strebsam ambitious, industrious
die **Strecke, -n** distance
das **Streichholz, ⁻er** match
(sich) **streiten, stritt (sich), (sich) gestritten** to quarrel, argue
der **Streß** stress
die **Strickwaren** *(pl.)* knitware
der **Strumpf, ⁻e** sock, stocking; hose
die **Strumpfhose, -n** panty hose
das **Stück, -e** piece
der **Student, -en, -en** student *(masc.)*
der **Studentenausweis, -e** student I.D.
das **Studentenheim, -e** dormitory
das **Studentenwerk, -e** student association
die **Studentin, -nen** student *(fem.)*
das **Studienbuch, ⁻er** record book of courses taken at a German university
der **Studiengang, ⁻e** course of study
studieren to study (at a university)
das **Studium, -ien** study, course work
der **Stuhl, ⁻e** chair
die **Stunde, -n** hour
der **Stundenplan, ⁻e** schedule
der **Sturm, ⁻e** storm
die **Suche, -n** search; **auf der Suche nach** in search of
suchen to look for, seek
der **Süden** south
südlich south, southern, southernly
der **Supermarkt, ⁻e** supermarket
sympatisch congenial, likeable
das **System, -e** system
die **Szene, -n** scene

T _____

die **Tabakwaren** *(pl.)* tobacco articles
die **Tafel, -n** blackboard
der **Tag, -e** day; **jeden Tag** every day
die **Tagesschau** "news and views"

die **Tagestemperatur, -en** daytime temperature

die **Tageszeit, -en** time of day

täglich daily

tagsüber in the daytime

der **Tank, -s** tank

tanken to get gasoline

die **Tankstelle, -n** gas station

der **Tankwart, -e** service station attendant

die **Tante, -n** aunt

tanzen to dance

die **Tasche, -n** purse, handbag; pocket

der **Tausendfüßler, –** centipede

das **Taxi, -s** taxicab

der **Taxifahrer, –** taxi driver *(masc.)*

die **Taxifahrerin, -nen** taxi driver *(fem.)*

das **Team, -s** team

die **Technik, -en** technology

die **Technik** technical science

der **Techniker, –** technician

technisch technical

der **Tee** tea

der **Teenager, –** teenager

der **Teig** dough

der **Teil, -e** part

der **Teilbetrag, ⸚e** installment

teilen to share

das **Telefon, -e** telephone

der **Telefonanruf, -e** telephone call

telefonieren to telephone

telefonisch by telephone

die **Telefonistin, -nen** telephone operator *(fem.)*

die **Telefonnummer, -n** telephone number

die **Telefonzelle, -n** telephone booth

der **Teller, –** plate

temperamentvoll lively

die **Temperatur, -en** temperature

der **Teppich, -e** rug, carpet

die **Terrasse, -n** terrace

der **Test, -s** test

teuer expensive

das **Theater, –** theater

der **Theaterbesuch, -e** theater attendance

die **Theorie, -n** theory

das **Thermometer, –** thermometer

der **Thunfisch, -e** tuna fish

das **Tiefdruckgebiet, -e** low pressure area

die **Tiefsttemperatur, -en** lowest temperature

das **Tier, -e** animal

der **Tisch, -e** table

die **Tischdecke, -n** tablecloth

der **Tischler, –** cabinetmaker

der **Toast** toast

toasten to toast

die **Tochter, ⸚** daughter

der **Tod, -esfälle** death

die **Toilette, -n** toilet; **auf die Toilette gehen** to go to the bathroom; **Toilette machen** to get dressed

tolerant tolerant

toll crazy, neat (idiomatic)

die **Tomate, -n** tomato

das **Tonbandgerät, -e** tape recorder

der **Topf, ⸚e** pot

der **Topflappen, –** potholder

der **Tornado, -s** tornado

der **Tourist, -en, -en** tourist

tragbar portable

tragen (trägt), trug, getragen to carry, wear

das **Transportmittel, –** means of transportation

die **Traube, -n** grape

trauen *(+ dat.)* to trust

träumen to dream

treffen (trifft), traf, getroffen to meet; hit

die **Treppe, -n** steps

treten (tritt), trat, ist getreten to step, enter, walk

treu faithful

trinken, trank, getrunken to drink

das **Trinkgeld, -er** tip

trocknen to dry

der **Trockner, –** dryer

die **Tschechoslowakei** Czechoslovakia

das **T–Shirt, -s** T–Shirt

tüchtig qualified, skilled, proficient, efficient

tun, tat, getan to do

die **Tür, -en** door

die **Türkei** Turkey

turnen to do gymnastics

die **Tüte, -n** bag

der **TÜV (Technischer Überwachungsverein)** technical inspection association (German motor vehicles must undergo a vigorous technical inspection every two years.)

der **Typ, -en** model, type

U

die **U–Bahn (Untergrundbahn), -en** subway

überein·stimmen to agree

sich **überlegen** to consider

übernachten to stay overnight

übernehmen (übernimmt), übernahm, übernommen to take over, assume

überprüfen to test, examine

überqueren to cross over; **die Straße überqueren** to cross the street
überwiegend predominant
üblich customary
die **Übung, -en** exercise, practice, class for exercises and discussion
die **Uhr, -en** clock, watch; **um wieviel Uhr?** at what time?
um·knicken to snap off
der **Umstand, ⸚e** circumstance
die **Umwelt** environment
um·ziehen, zog um, ist umgezogen to move (domicile)
die **Unbequemlichkeit, -en** discomfort
unberechtigt unjustified
unentbehrlich indispensable
unerfahren inexperienced
der **Unfall, ⸚e** accident
unfallfrei free of accidents
Ungarn Hungary
ungefähr approximately
ungenügend unsatisfactory
ungerecht unfair
ungestört undisturbed
das **Unglück** misfortune
die **Uniform, -en** uniform
die **Universität, -en (die Uni, -s)** university; **an der Uni** at the university
unsicher uncertain
die **Unterbringung** accommodation
untergebracht to be housed, arranged
sich **unterhalten (unterhält sich), unterhielt sich, sich unterhalten** to entertain oneself, to converse
unterhaltsam amusing, entertaining
die **Unterhaltung, -en** conversation, entertainment
die **Unterhaltungslektüre, -n** popular literature
die **Unterhaltungsmusik** popular music
die **Unterhaltungssendung, -en** entertainment program
unter·heben, hob unter, unterhoben to fold in
unterscheiden, unterschied, unterschieden to distinguish
sich **unterscheiden, unterschied sich, sich unterschieden** to differ
der **Unterschied, -e** difference
unterschreiben, unterschrieb, unterschrieben to sign
die **Unterschrift, -en** signature
die **Unterzeichnung, -en** signature
das **Unwetter, –** bad weather
die **Unzuverlässigkeit** undependability
der **Urlaub, -e** vacation

das **Urlaubsgeld, -er** vacation money
das **Urteil, -e** judgment

V

der **Vater, ⸚** father
verantwortungsbewußt responsible
verbilligt reduced in price
die **Verbindung, -en** connection; **sich in Verbindung setzen (mit)** to contact
das **Verbindungshaus, ⸚er** fraternity house
verbittert bitter
verbringen, verbrachte, verbracht to spend (time)
verderben (verdirbt), verdarb, verdorben to destroy
verdienen to earn
die **Vereinbarung, -en** agreement, arrangement
die **Vereinigten Staaten** United States
sich **verfahren (verfährt sich), verfuhr sich, sich verfahren** to get lost
verfolgen to pursue, persecute
vergehen, verging, ist vergangen to pass away, perish
vergessen (vergißt), vergaß, vergessen to forget
vergiften to poison
der **Vergleich, -e** comparison
vergleichen, verglich, verglichen to compare
die **Vergnügung, -en** pleasure
das **Verhältnis -se** relationship
das **Verhandlungsgeschick** skill in negotiation
der **Verkauf, ⸚e** sale
verkaufen to sell
der **Verkäufer, –** salesman, vendor
die **Verkäuferin, -nen** saleslady
die **Verkaufsabteilung, -en** sales department
die **Verkehrsampel, -n** traffic light
das **Verkehrsbüro, -s** information bureau
verknallen: sich in jemanden verknallen *(colloq.)* to fall in love with someone
verlassen (verläßt) verließ, verlassen to leave, abandon, forsake
sich **verlassen (verläßt sich), verließ sich, sich verlassen auf** *(+ acc.)* to rely on
verleihen, verlieh, verliehen to rent out, bestow, give
verlieben: sich in jemanden verlieben to fall in love with someone

200

verlieren, verlor, verloren to lose

die **Verlobungsfeier, -n** engagement celebration

der **Verlobungsring, -e** engagement ring

vermissen to miss

vermitteln to secure for

vermutlich probably

verrühren to mix

verschieden different, various

verschwinden, verschwand, ist verschwunden to disappear

versichern to assure

die **Versicherung, -en** insurance

versiegeln to seal

das **Verständnis** sympathetic understanding

verständnisvoll understanding

verteidigen to defend

der **Vertrag, ⁻e** contract

vertrauen *(+ dat.)* to trust

vertraulich confidential, intimate

vertreten (vertritt), vertrat, vertreten to represent

verurteilen to condemn; **zum Tode verurteilen** to condemn to death

verwalten to supervise

der **Verwandte, -n, -n** relative

verwenden to use, apply

verwitwet widowed

verwöhnen to spoil

das **Verzeichnis, -se** index

verzichten auf *(+ acc.)* to forgo something

viertens fourthly

die **Volksschule, -n** German elementary school

der **Volkswagen (VW), –** Volkswagen (VW) (Note: All makes of cars are masculine in gender.)

die **Volkswirtschaft** economics

vollausgestattet all options, fully equipped

das **Vollkornbrot** wholemeal bread

vollständig complete

vorbei·gehen, ging vorbei, ist vorbeigegangen to go past; **vorbeigehen an** *(+ dat.)* to go by

vorbildlich ideal

der **Vorgang, ⁻e** incident, event

vor·haben to plan

der **Vorhang, ⁻e** curtain

vor·lesen (liest vor), las vor, vorgelesen to read aloud

die **Vorlesung, -en** lecture, lecture course; **eine Vorlesung halten** to give a lecture; **eine Vorlesung hören** to attend a lecture

das **Vorlesungsverzeichnis, -se** course catalog

vor·machen to put or place before; **jemandem etwas vormachen** to take in, fool

der **Vorname, -ns, -n** first name

der **Vorschlag, ⁻e** suggestion

vor·schlagen (schlägt vor), schlug vor, vorgeschlagen to suggest

vor·schreiben, schrieb vor, vorgeschrieben to prescribe

die **Vorsicht** precaution, care; **Vorsicht!** Be careful!

die **Vorspeise, -n** appetizer

sich **vor·stellen** *(+ acc.)* to imagine

der **Vorteil, -e** advantage

vorteilhaft advantageous

vor·ziehen, zog vor, vorgezogen to prefer

der **Vorzug, ⁻e** preference

W

die **Waage, -n** scale

der **Wachtmeister, –** policeman, sergeant-major; **Herr Wachtmeister!** Officer!

der **Wagen, –** automobile; car of a train

wählen to choose

wahrscheinlich probably

die **Währung, -en** currency

der **Wald, ⁻er** forest

die **Wand, ⁻e** wall

wandern to hike

das **Wandern** hiking

die **Ware, -n** article, good, ware, product

das **Warenhaus, ⁻er** department store

die **Wärme** warmth

die **Warmfront, -en** warm front

warnen to warn; **warnen vor** *(+ dat.)* to warn of

warten to wait; **warten auf** *(+ acc.)* to wait for

der **Wartesaal, -säle** waiting room

das **Waschbecken, –** sink

die **Wäsche** washing, wash, linens

waschen (wäscht), wusch, gewaschen to wash

sich **waschen (wäscht sich), wusch sich, sich gewaschen** to wash; **Ich wasche mir die Hände.** I'm washing my hands.

die **Waschküche, -n** washer–dryer area, area to hang up clothes to dry

die **Waschmaschine, -n** washing–machine

das **WC, -s (das Wasserklosett, -s)** toilet, washroom

wechseln to change; **das Öl wechseln** to change the oil

der **Wecker, –** alarm clock

der **Weg, -e** way, path; **den Weg zeigen** to give directions

weg·laufen (läuft weg), lief weg, ist weggelaufen to run away

weg·ziehen, zog weg, ist weggezogen to move away

der **Wehrdienst** military service

das **Weib, -er** *(archaic)* woman

weiblich female

weich soft

weichgekocht soft boiled

das **Weihnachtsgeld** Christmas money

der **Wein, -e** wine

die **Weißwurst, ⸚e** white sausage

weit far

weiter further

wenig little, few

das **Werbeplakat, -e** advertisement poster

die **Werbung, -en** advertisement, publicity

die **Werkstattrechnung, -en** repair shop bill

der **Werktag, -e** weekday

das **Werkzeug, -e** tool

wertvoll worthwhile

weshalb why, for what reason

der **Westen** west, West

westlich west, westerly, western

der **Wettbewerb, -e** contest

das **Wetter** weather

das **Wetteramt, ⸚er** weather bureau

das **Wettergebiet, -e** weather area

die **Wetterkarte, -n** weather map

die **Wettervorhersage, -n** weather forecast

wichtig important

wiegen, wog, gewogen to weigh

Wien Vienna

das **Wienerwürstl, –** (Bavarian dialect) frankfurter

willkommen welcome

der **Wind, -e** wind

die **Windschutzscheibe, -n** windshield

der **Winter, –** winter

der **Winterreifen, –** snow tire

wirken auf *(+ acc.)* to affect, act on

wirklich really

der **Wirt, -e** innkeeper *(masc.)*

die **Wirtin, -nen** innkeeper *(fem.)*

das **Wischblatt, ⸚er** windshield wiper blade

wissen (weiß), wußte, gewußt to know (a fact, but not in the sense of knowing a person, place or object)

die **Wissenschaft, -en** science

der **Wissenschaftler, –** scientist

wissenschaftlich scientific

die **Witwe, -n** widow

der **Witwer, –** widower

die **Woche, -n** week; **in der Woche** per week, every week

das **Wochenende, -n** weekend; **am Wochenende** on the weekend

der **Wochenlohn, ⸚e** weekly wages

der **Wochentag, -e** weekday

wochentags weekdays

woher where from, from what place

wohin where to, to what place

wohl well; indeed; probably

wohlproportioniert well–proportioned

wohnen to live

wohnhaft domicile, dwelling, living; **wohnhaft bei** care of (c/o); **wohnhaft in** domicile in

die **Wohnstube, -n** family room

die **Wohnung, -en** apartment

die **Wohnwand, ⸚e** wall-length set of cabinets for living room

die **Wolke, -n** cloud

die **Wolkendecke, -n** cloud cover

wolkenlos cloudless

wolkig cloudy

das **Wörterverzeichnis, -se** vocabulary list

der **Wortschatz** vocabulary

wunderschön gorgeous, beautiful

wünschen to wish

die **Wurst, ⸚e** sausage

Z

zahlen to pay

die **Zahlung, -en** payment; **in Zahlung geben** to trade in

der **Zahn, ⸚e** tooth; **sich die Zähne putzen** to brush one's teeth

die **Zapfsäule, -n** gas pump

der **Zebrastreifen, –** stripes (on a street crossing)

das **Zeichen, –** symbol, sign

zeichnen to designate, characterize

die **Zeit, -en** time; **zur Zeit** at the time

die **Zeitkarte, -n** season ticket

der **Zeitraum, ⸚e** period of time

die **Zeitschrift, -en** magazine

die **Zeitung, -en** newspaper

zeitweise at times, from time to time

zentral central

die **Zentralheizung, -en** central heating

die **Zentralverriegelung, -en** central locking device in a car der **Zettel,** – note

das **Zeugnis, -se** report card

ziehen, zog, hat gezogen to pull, draw

der **Zielbahnhof, ⸚e** station of destination

die **Zielstrebigkeit** resoluteness

ziemlich rather, pretty much

die **Zigarette, -n** cigarette

das **Zimmer,** – room

der **Zimmerkollege, -n** roommate (*masc.*)

die **Zimmerkollegin, -nen** roommate (*fem.*)

der **Zimmernachweis, -e** room information

der **Zimmerpreis, -e** price for a room

der **Zimt** cinnamon

zischen to hiss

die **Zitrone, -n** lemon

der **Zoll, ⸚e** tariff, customs, duty; **durch den Zoll gehen** to go through customs

zu·bereiten to prepare

die **Zubereitung, -en** preparation

der **Zucker** sugar

zuerst at first

zufrieden satisfied

der **Zug, ⸚e** train

zu·gehen, ging zu, zugegangen auf (*+ acc.*) to approach

zugleich at the same time

zu·hören (*+ dat.*) to listen to

zukünftig future

zuletzt finally, in the end

der **Zünder,** – fuse

die **Zündkerze, -n** spark plug

der **Zungenbrecher,** – tongue twister

sich **zurecht·finden, fand sich zurecht, sich zurechtgefunden** to find one's way

sich **zusammen·brauen** to brew together (storms)

der **Zusammenhang, ⸚e** connection

zuverlässig dependable

der **Zweck, -e** aim, purpose

zwei two; **zu zweit** together, by two's

der **Zweig, -e** branch

zweitens secondly

zweitklassig second class

die **Zwetschge, -n** (Swiss, Austrian, south German dialect) damson, plum

die **Zwischenprüfung, -en** mid–curriculum exam

zwitschern to twitter, chirp